RAVISH KUMAR is among India's leading journalists and public intellectuals. He was Senior Executive Editor with NDTV for several years before he resigned in late 2022 on moral grounds. He now runs an immensely popular and influential news channel on YouTube. He is the recipient of the Ramon Magsaysay Award (2019), the Ramnath Goenka Award for Excellence in Journalism in (2017), the inaugural Kuldip Nayar Journalism Award (2017) and the Ganesh Shankar Vidyarthi Award for Hindi Journalism and Creative Writing (2010). His other books include *Ishq Mein Shahar Hona* (*A City Happens in Love*) and *Dekhte Rahiye*.

Praise for *The Free Voice*

'Kumar's India is not in the least pretty, it is a country of a brutal and fearful citizenry and he obsessively speaks of the need to seek a better world, a nation that is free of hatred and violence... *The Free Voice* is passionate, sincere and strikes a chord, and will hopefully open up debate on the way forward.'—Geeta Seshu, *Biblio*

'Ravish Kumar's book highlights...how the fear of institutional, physical and psychological violence is being used to replace debate, dialogue and social harmony...A journalist is not supposed to be a fence-sitter; he is supposed to take sides. Irrespective of whether one agrees with his views or not, it cannot be denied that Ravish Kumar excels in his pursuit as a journalist. The lines from Hindi poet Ramdhari Singh Dinkar sum up his endeavour: "Samar sesh hai nahin paap ka bhagi kewal vyaghra, jo tatastha hai samay likhega unka bhi apradh." (It is not the evil-doer alone who is to blame, all those who are indifferent are equal sinners).'—Sandeep Sinha, *The Tribune*

'Ravish Kumar reminds us on every page of the dangers that people face today. He poses a simple question: Should you report the truth and run the risk of being dubbed peddler of fake news, or should you settle down to being a cheerleader of the government in power and win praise? In settling down for the former, Kumar puts himself out for being singled out by the government…[This book] is a mirror of our times.'—Anuradha Raman, *The Hindu*

'[*The Free Voice*] needs to be read, engaged with and discussed at great length. This is a book that every opinion maker and journalist should read carefully, and be inspired.'—Chitra Ahanthem, *Imphal Free Press*

'*The Free Voice* serves both as a mirror and siren. On the one hand, it reflects the complex social realities in the country today without the least exaggeration. On the other, it warns citizens of the dire consequences of the deification of political leaders and the further erosion of democratic and constitutional values. [T]his is a must-read for students, social scientists, activists and, more importantly, citizens, who should be concerned with upholding democratic values and institutions no matter which government is voted into power.'—Aishwarya Bhuta, *LSE Review of Books*

THE FREE VOICE

ON DEMOCRACY, CULTURE AND THE NATION

RAVISH KUMAR

Translated from the Hindi by
Chitra Padmanabhan, Anurag Basnet and Ravi Singh

SPEAKING TIGER

SPEAKING TIGER BOOKS LLP
125A Ground Floor, Shahpur Jat,
New Delhi – 110049

First published in India in hardcover by Speaking Tiger 2018
This revised edition published in 2024

ISBN: 978-93-89231-19-9

10 9 8 7 6 5 4 3 2 1

Typeset in Bembo Std by SÜRYA, New Delhi
Printed at Chaman Enterprises, New Delhi

Contents

Preface to the 2024 Edition

When this book was first published, in early 2018, the foundation of a new edifice of lies was being laid in India's democracy. Since then, not one but many vast buildings have been built on that foundation. A Smart City of Politics has risen, where the rule of the majority that remains silent has been established. This silence needs to be recognized. I am not talking of those who have been silenced; I am not talking of the silence born of fear, but the silence born of consent. This majority isn't just silent about every wrong that is committed, it has also shut its ears to any questions that are asked. The wilful silence of this majority is a wall that has been used to exclude from our democracy all those who ask for information and accountability. This society has stopped listening to those who speak. It has stopped reading them. It listens only to Power.

The Smart City of Politics is also the Smart City of Lies. This complex has grown far bigger than the project that was launched in 2014. It does not matter now whether any city in the country has actually become 'smart'; the silent-by-choice majority has accepted the Smart City of Lies as its shining future. It does not matter if the Hindu Nation has not yet been formally announced; the nationalism of the Smart City of Lies *is* Hindu nationalism. But we must not mistake the character of this enormous City for Hinduism—its religion is Modi. Narendra Modi is its Shankaracharya. Indian democracy has been brought to a place that many had feared for decades it would reach. The journey has not taken even a full ten years.

As I write this Preface, four Shankaracharyas of the country have refused to participate in the Pran Pratishtha ritual of the Ram temple in Ayodhya. The vile language that is being used by the IT Cell to troll the Shankaracharyas, and the fact that there is no outrage over this in the Smart City of Lies, is proof that along with democracy, faith, too, has been hijacked. Henceforth, nothing shall be what it is meant to be. Our democracy has been replaced by a theocracy at whose head, as Shankaracharya and Dharmacharya, is Narendra Modi. Religion, which bowed to no authority, has also been captured and quelled.

The visual order of our democracy has been changed in such a manner that it is no longer possible to see politics and religion separately. When we look at any act of politics or governance now, we will see it clothed in the robes of religion—a particular religion. The symbols, images, names and institutions which defined India's democracy are no longer visible. New structures have come up as markers of democracy. I call it the new visual order, where the nation's leader looks like a national priest, not a prime minister. So, when the four Shankaracharyas refused to attend the inauguration of the Ram temple, they were thrown out of the freshly-minted theocracy. The deity cannot be installed in a temple that is still under construction. This is what Hindu tradition says. The Ram temple is still under construction, why is an incomplete temple being inaugurated? The media of India's new theocracy crushed this question, because asking questions about religious traditions is regarded as asking questions of Modi. To question Modi is a crime in the new order. The punishment is not always jail; the biggest punishment is that the society under this theocracy expels you. It stops listening to you. It blots you out. This is the rule in the Smart City of Lies.

Our democracy is now a vassal of the theocratic state. In this democracy, there is a new path to absolution for every Constitutional sin: praise of Modi; worship of Modi. With a daily dip in this river of devotion, hundreds of judges, governors, bureaucrats and journalists are cleansing themselves of their Constitutional sins. To the majority in this theocratic state, these sins are of no consequence. To these citizens, the Constitution that *makes* them citizens is of no consequence. It isn't sacred. It isn't immortal. Only the Sanatan Hindu soul that has submitted to the chief priest is immortal. The soul of the Constitution may die; it is of no consequence. There was a time when religion was the path to seek forgiveness and cleanse oneself of sin. Now religion is being used to cover up sins and lies. This is what happens to religion in a theocracy.

In the Smart City of Lies, the WhatsApp groups of housing societies are the largest media network. It is here that news is manufactured, distorted and broadcast more widely than through any other network. But a researcher would find very little information about these groups. This network of WhatsApp groups does not want to know anything outside the rules of its theocracy. It obediently follows every order given by the chief priest of their faith. Through this network of countless WhatsApp groups, every life is monitored 24x7: what someone is reading, watching, saying, thinking. How many diyas are being lit and how many thalis banged; how many flags of the theocracy are being hoisted on balconies and rooftops. The members of this WhatsApp society post the same content every morning, and all day, to prove their loyalty. They have won the Great War against

'Good Morning'—it has been slayed and replaced with 'Suprabhat' and 'Surya Namaskar' and 'NaMo NaMo'. The world has been brought to its knees by the 'Vishwaguru'. The world, of course, does not know it has been defeated.

The WhatsApp groups, immersed in the celebration of their victory, no longer want any information which will question the mythologies of their theocracy and their chief priest. They do not want a media whose journalists will question and disprove the claims of Narendra Modi's government. These certified citizens of the Smart City of Lies hear only what Modi ji says. They see only what Modi ji shows them. This gives them such power that they can prove any lie as true. Truth is the biggest Lie. When this state has been reached, all is bliss. A new happiness has been born, which I call Hindu Happiness. The certified citizens of the theocracy, the Smart City of Lies have attained Hindu happiness. They no longer have anything to do with the sorrows of politics, the sorrows of this world. It is futile to expect them to mourn the death of democracy.

The first structures of the Smart City of Lies were coming up when this book was being written. Today, as

I write the introduction to this new edition, that City is a sprawling, seething, shouting landscape of towers. Towers of untruth and noise. Every day, the subjects of this book are being updated outside the book. We know far less about our democracy than we did before. Few seem to regret this.

If you want to understand Indian democracy, then take a look at India's newspapers and news channels. The vast profession of journalism was crushed before our eyes. For years, hundreds of thousands of young people studied journalism and dreamt of joining this profession—they dreamt of investigating, speaking, asking questions. Today, there are many schools and colleges of journalism, but there are no institutions for journalists. Students of journalism will graduate with degrees and diplomas and find jobs in institutes that serve the politics of Prime Minister Narendra Modi. The media has become a recruitment agency for the BJP. As soon as you enter the media, you automatically become an employee of the BJP and Narendra Modi.

The pages of newspapers are empty of news. Instead, the Prime Minister fills these pages, well-groomed and immaculately dressed. He has filled the void in Indian journalism with himself. If he does not go to Ayodhya or Lakshadweep, the journalists, ceaseless chanters of his name, stare at empty days and nights. After 2014, the media was liberated of the need to worry about the state of our Republic. News died. The media shed the burdensome responsibility of being the fourth pillar of democracy. India's mainstream media should be given credit for playing the most active role in the fall of our democracy. It has been celebrating the passing of democracy even before the formal announcement of the assassination. It is no longer necessary to ask these journalists: what is your story, what is your news? Everyone has the same news: PM Modi and his New India. These journalists have taken upon themselves the responsibility of protecting this New India and its new religion and chief priest.

And yet, none of the TV channels that chant Modi's name all day and all night have kept a count of how many dresses the Prime Minister has worn in the nearly ten years that he has been in office. Nor has there been any classification of his costumes by colour and design. Surely these designer journalists can bring their skills to the subject of the PM's wardrobe? This should be a matter close to their hearts. The PM wears new, splendidly cut dresses every day. There must be some arrangement for sewing these clothes. Are fresh sets of clothes laid out for selection before the Prime Minister every day? Or is an entire inventory displayed before him on the last day of every month to select dresses for the following thirty days? How many dresses are rejected? How many alterations are done? Has the Prime Minister worn all the clothes he has selected for any given month? Has the Prime Minister repeated any dress in ten years? What happens to the clothes he never wears, or to those that he wears once and discards? Are they given away to fans? Are they set aside for a museum that must certainly be in the making? We don't know.

What does this tell us about our media, which lives and breathes and rolls over for the PM? If PM Modi is the only news in this country, isn't it surprising how little information his poodle media has about him? Today's India knows next to nothing about the prime minister whom it sees every hour of every day. He, on the other hand, knows almost everything about almost everyone.

It isn't as if every voice has fallen silent. But those who should listen have decided that they will not do so. There are still some journalists left, only a handful, who take great pains to dig out news, even though the price that must be paid for this audacity is now very high. They are risking their well-being and security, and sometimes their lives, to save a profession which has given up the belief that journalism cannot exist without conviction and fearlessness. The last ten years in India have proved that even slavery can be journalism. There is no need to be bold and truthful to be a journalist. In fact, journalism no longer requires you to be a journalist. When this medium is dead, how will the voice of the public be heard? We, the people, have buried this question. We have changed the very meaning of what it is to be a reader and a viewer. We do not want to hear our voice, we only want to hear Modi's voice. We do not want to read newspapers for news of our world and our lives, we want to read them for praise of Modi. Meanwhile, the handful who still attempt journalism have been locked away in the furthest, darkest corner of a big house where The Master's voice echoes day and night.

This hasn't happened in India alone. Across the world, newspapers and news channels have morphed into pamphlets and instruments of state propaganda. Almost every house of journalism has been demolished. Israel's attack on Gaza has brought global institutions of journalism to their knees. Institutions that were far from Israel's reach have also bowed before it. When South Africa accused Israel of genocide in the International Court of Justice, most international news channels did not broadcast the news. When Israel responded to the charge with brazen lies and arrogance, the same channels broadcast its bullying rebuttal. This is exactly what happens in India. When the opposition speaks, it is made to disappear. That the Prime Minister is fasting, ahead of his inauguration of the temple in Ayodhya, is the only headline news.

Journalism has been trampled upon everywhere. No one in any country has any reference point today for what journalism should really be; what it had once been. By joining hands with power, Indian and global institutions of journalism have become complicit in the crimes of Power. They haven't arrived at this station as reluctant travellers or abductees. They made a conscious choice to become the henchmen of Power.

And yet, we must *not* look at the Indian media's decline as any ordinary story of decline in a post-truth world. We must also look at its weaponization and criminalization. We must look at the manner in which the Indian media has consistently targeted a specific community, as well as the opposition; how it has become the mouthpiece for the government and also its private militia. This had never happened before. Never in the history of the Indian Republic had the media merged with the political imaginary of a 'Hindu nation', its professionalism supplanted by 'Hindu nationalism'.

The anchors of news channels with the 'highest TRP ratings' loudly defend the government at every opportunity. But when there is serious news, when the government should act, and should be hauled over the coals when it does not, these anchors are all silent. I will give you two recent examples. The first is from PM Modi's electoral constituency, Banaras. IIT, Banaras Hindu University is among the leading educational institutions of the country. Here, three men were accused of molesting and gangraping a female student at gunpoint on the night of 1 November 2023. There are credible reports that the police already knew the identity of these three men when students of the University demonstrated in large numbers on 2 November, demanding action. But the men were arrested only after sixty days, and it was revealed that they are part of the ruling BJP's IT Cell. There was no serious media investigation, either, for two months. Some newspapers reported the matter *after* the arrest of the men. But the mainstream TV anchors have had nothing to say.

A second example: Two Hindu boys adopted fake Muslim names and sent emails that they would blow up the Ram temple in Ayodhya. The police arrested them, but there has been zero debate in the mainstream media on the extremely dangerous larger implications of this.

There are numerous such examples. All of them in stark contrast to the aggression and sensationalism that the news anchors unleash when a criminal or an accused is Muslim, or when they decide to pillory the opposition parties for faults real or imagined. This is a clear sign that the Indian mainstream media is no longer a stakeholder in India's democracy.

This makes no difference to the crores who have merged themselves with the Leader and the Party. The rest of us have all become mere spectators of the massive defeat of our beliefs. Even those of us who saw the dark night approaching and have tried for ten years to speak of our apprehensions to every home, even the homes that had shut their doors on us.

In 2024, our apprehensions will probably come true. The land around us is rapidly turning into an island; an ocean that is growing bigger by the day surrounds us. But this is a great moment for all those who have been declared crushed and defeated. This is their moment—the few who paid a price, big or small, for refusing to bow down, for holding their head high and speaking out in private and public spaces. They keep speaking, hoping someone, somewhere will hear them. And if no one does, they know they must still speak. Speak to themselves, listen to themselves.

Stand tall on this side and look at the other side. And speak. This much, if nothing more, to remind yourself that you have a voice: Hello. Mic testing. Check, check, check. One, two, three. Check.

I realize this mic testing will go on for a very long time. Keep at it. Keep testing your voice.

RAVISH KUMAR
New Delhi, 14 January 2024

Preface to the 2019 Edition

It is 2019. A new world is truly upon us. As I begin this message, I receive a WhatsApp message in Hindi, written in the English alphabet: 'Aaj teri leanching ki jayegi.' ('You will be leanched [sic] today.') Some of us—or, let us hope, many of us—may still be horrified by a lynching, but for some others it appears to have become a routine act. It is now quite normal to think of lynching anyone you disagree with; anyone who is outnumbered. In Jharkhand, on June 17, a young man called Tabrez Ansari was tied to a pole sometime around midnight and beaten by a mob till six in the morning. The police arrived late, which is usual. Tabrez was taken to hospital, where even his blood pressure wasn't recorded. He died four days later.

It was a similar mob that chased and killed Inspector Subodh Kumar Singh in Bulandshahr, on the outskirts of Delhi. He was trying to control a mob that had gone on the rampage after cow carcasses were discovered in a nearby jungle. This was in December 2018. Back then, such things were done in the name of the cow. When reports began to come in that cows were starving to death in official shelters, that stray cattle were destroying crops and farmers were angry, politics abandoned the cow. But the project of fear and violence that had been started in its name continues. The slogan 'Jai Shri Ram' has replaced the cow. As he was being battered, Tabrez Ansari was asked to say 'Jai Shri Ram'. He did. It did not save him.

'Mob' isn't just a word. It is made up of tens, hundreds, thousands of people. People who beat and kill; who record the beating and killing on their phones; who stand and watch and do not speak. They don't speak even when dozens of young men of their own community become killers, or when they are no longer useful as foot soldiers and are put in jail or on trial for assault and murder. Roving mobs are being manufactured with great speed. It is no longer possible to know where a mob might gather, or when.

It was no ordinary event when shouts of 'Jai Shri Ram' rang in the Lok Sabha as Asaduddin Owaisi, an elected Member of Parliament, took his oath. The slogan wasn't spoken for the love of Ram. It was spoken to intimidate and mock Owaisi, who responded with 'Allah O Akbar'. The provocation and the reaction were both expunged from the proceedings of the Lok Sabha, but the episode became both an affirmation of and a call for proceedings in the streets. Communalism is being legitimized as patriotism. In the drawing rooms of the elite, communal talk is already like dessert after a good dinner. Bigotry isn't always shabbily dressed; it also wears the robes of high culture. The modestly educated, the unemployed and underemployed, lack the skill to craft impressive sentences and arguments. They hammer in plain sight. Unlike those who are educated and gainfully employed; who realize that personally beating and killing people can sometimes be harmful. So they speak in a low voice and sophisticated sentences in support of the politics of fixing a group or community, of teaching it a lesson. We call them good people, reasonable people.

None of this is new, it has happened before in India and elsewhere. And yet, a lot is happening in ways that are entirely new. A leading TV channel tells us that India will win the 2019 Cricket World Cup because of Prime Minister Narendra Modi's luck. The news anchor's high-decibel voice echoes in lakhs of homes, and it becomes part of elite discourse. At the same time, there is other news: unemployment reaches record levels as the economy slows down; encephalitis kills 140 children in Muzzafarpur, Bihar; seven men die cleaning sewers in Gujarat. News channels are silent about the Prime Minister's luck, or indeed his intervention, in these cases. The crores of people who watch these channels know what good journalism should be, but they appear to have aligned themselves with meaningless journalism.

In the end, the PM's luck could not prevent India's loss in the World Cup. But it does ensure good times for the anchors of popular TV channels. These talking heads don't practice anything that even remotely resembles journalism, but they have become the face of Indian journalism. They are no longer answerable to anyone except the ruling establishment. They only need to appear on the TV screen every evening and arrange a shouting match between rival spokespersons, and obliterate news altogether. This disorder is now so widespread that it is futile to expect ethics or integrity. Bad journalism never had the kind of credibility that it has today. News channels have worked tirelessly to kill India's democratic ideals, with the result that vast numbers of the Indian people follow channels that ask no questions of the government. These channels have trained their viewers to watch only a particular kind of TV where nothing is demanded of them, except a willing and complete suspension of belief. And absolute amorality. Elected representatives can garland killers, ministers can lie, news anchors can read out government press releases as news. It bothers no one enough.

After the first budget of the re-elected BJP government, the Finance Ministry barred journalists from entering its offices without prior permission. Before this order, any journalist with a Press Information Bureau (PIB) card could visit the Ministry, meet anyone there and come back and file a story. This was how Somesh Jha was able to do a story for the *Business Standard* about a report—suppressed by the government—that the level of unemployment in India during 2017-18 was the highest in forty-five years.

No such news story will now be possible. The Finance Ministry tells us that the waiting area for journalists has been spruced up, they will be made very comfortable. But they can enter the hallowed offices only after they have secured an appointment with a senior officer. The Editors Guild has criticized the move. The people of India have chosen to look the other way. They had been similarly unconcerned when, during the elections of 2019, the mainstream media was awash with news in praise of a certain political party and a single leader. No questions were asked when, in the vast, diverse and great democracy that is India, the entire opposition was made invisible. You couldn't expect anything of the Election Commission, either; it was being routinely accused of bias. And when it took no cognizance of the Prime Minister's repeated violation of the model code of conduct, the Commission proved that it had read the sign of the times: neutrality has little value. We have paid the price for this kind of thing in the past, but no one fears history anymore. History can be easily changed. Events and personalities can be erased from the collective memory of the nation, just as easily as they can be erased from school textbooks.

The press as an instrument of official propaganda is now a plain fact of our democratic system. News is suppressed, manipulated, manufactured with impunity. The Indian people never had much agency, but even the little that they did have they seem to have surrendered to powers about whose true intentions they know next to nothing. Perhaps at no other time in the history of the independent nation has there been this degree of faith in political authority and such an appetite for non-news and fake news. In the World Press Freedom index, India ranks 140 among 180 nations. The government alone isn't responsible for this. Audiences and readers too have put us there: channels and newspapers that sing hosannas in praise of the government day after day have the highest ratings and subscriptions.

The Indian government's own draft education policy tells us that the National Assessment and Accreditation Council (NAAC) rates sixty-eight per cent of our universities as average or below average. Ninety-one per cent of colleges are rated average or below average. These second- and third-rate colleges would have produced generations of average or below average students and scholars. A great deal of hard work must have gone into finishing off all curiosity, any hunger for knowledge and information. The youth of today's India have been in the making for decades. The youth themselves are not to blame. Except that they were asleep when the tragic farce was being scripted, and they remain asleep now that the project of their enfeeblement and enslavement is complete. The young no longer want to understand why a system made them spend lakhs of rupees studying to be engineers when at the end of it all they could not find jobs that would pay them even ten thousand. Young Indians don't question why scores of engineering colleges were set up and then shut down. They took loans to gain admission and study in colleges that promised them training and placements. Those colleges don't exist anymore, but the loans are still being repaid. Meanwhile, a sweat-shop army of software engineers is slaving away in the IT cell of our new rulers. These young men and women will never be part of the glorious national history that they've been employed to construct with lies, hate, abuse and character assassination. Just as their colleges disappeared overnight, they will be thrown into the dark basement of this so-called glorious history.

Democracies are created and sustained by idealists who seek to understand their world; who demand information and question the status quo. Can we expect such democratic ideals from the youth of a country where ninety-one per cent of colleges are average or below average? Sixty-five per cent of Indians may well be under the age of thirty-five, but there's little sign of anything fresh in their thinking. Their minds aren't young. They were first burdened with great ignorance, and now they've been blinded by communalism. We speak of economic and social inequality, but we must also recognize the inequality of knowledge in India. Knowledge inequality is now so deep that a good book, a good debate isn't going to fix it. An overwhelming majority of our young people only understand the language of powerpoint and 140-character tweets; their powers of comprehension haven't been allowed to develop beyond this.

With ninety-one per cent of the country's colleges being second- and third-rate, it was inevitable that a great abyss would separate its students from the realm of knowledge. This must be the reason why the WhatsApp university became so popular in India. Its shiny memes were like pages of a new, undemanding book that explained the world to them in thrilling images and minimum words. The scholars and intellectuals of our big cities rarely spoke of the immense injustice that had been done, and continues to be done, to these crores of young people across India. The few scholars who did speak of it had already been marginalized in academia as socialists and anti-nationals. The young were impatient to learn and feel a little less disempowered, but every means of acquiring knowledge had been broken. For the first time, the WhatsApp university gave them the pride of knowing things. Lies and misleading information designed to prejudice them and incite them to violence began to reach their smartphones as personal messages. It was the home delivery of knowledge. The young recipient of such information finally began to feel empowered. He hadn't found truth to feel proud about, so he began to take pride in falsehood. A part of him knew that it was falsehood, no better than the ignorance he had been condemned to before, and so his pride became irrational, prickly; a weapon to bludgeon his critics with.

You need knowledge in order to become citizens in the fullest sense and speak truth to power. When every effort to know the truth is thwarted by withholding information or spreading lies, the regular practice of speaking out is slowly lost. News gathered after rigorous research and investigation stokes the desire to know more. Such news began to disappear from Indian news channels and papers some years ago. Hindi newspapers, especially, have worked hard to keep the young exactly as their ninety-one per cent average and below average colleges had shaped them. People believe the press is giving them information, but most mainstream media organizations tell us only what they are instructed to tell us. Authority knows that when people have information, they speak out. So the media has been bought over or conscripted into the project of broadcasting lies or selective information, so that people's ability to confront authority and ask questions is diminished. Parents tell their children not to speak or write too much. Teachers advise their students to study and 'not indulge in politics'. All of society has come together to make India's great democracy diffident and apprehensive.

In May 2019, Prime Minister Narendra Modi, seeking a second mandate from the people of India, gave one of his rare press interviews to Raj Kamal Jha and Ravish Tiwari of *The Indian Express*. At one point, he was asked whether he brooked dissent, and if he had ever been overruled in cabinet or party meetings.

> ...[F]ind out the average time of cabinet meetings during the Manmohan Singh government. The average time was 20 minutes. The average time of my cabinet meetings is three hours. What do you think happens over that time? There have been several cabinet proposals which have gone back. Several have been referred to a temporary GoM (group of ministers). Additionally, I have done meetings of my entire council of ministers where everyone is invited to speak and deliberate. Presentations are made, but these are not for media.
>
> **But what do we get as news?**
>
> That is your problem. I am not undemocratic. I have met 250 people in Delhi for three hours each of freewheeling discussions. I believe that the thinking of the government as well as the thinking of the people in media should be transparent. Whether news gets published is not the only thing in a democracy.

India's Prime Minister was talking here of changing the press and the government. Perhaps the Finance Ministry's order denying free access to journalists is an early indication of what the PM meant. 'Whether news gets published is not the only thing in a democracy.' It surprised me that even *The Indian Express* seemed to miss the significance of this line which should, really, have been a banner headline. Perhaps such oversight is not unusual.

Meanwhile, the Right to Information Act, which was one of the great achievements of our civil society, has been amended to bring the hitherto independent Chief Information Commissioner and Information Commissioners—both at the centre and in the states—under the direct control of the central government. No matter. Whether people get the information they want or not is not the only thing in a democracy.

The Lok Sabha has passed amendments to the Unlawful Activities Prevention Act that give authorities the power to declare any individual a 'terrorist'. The original Act already had many provisions to deal with people linked to terrorist organizations, even if all they could be accused of was possessing literature that might be deemed to be sympathetic to banned organizations. What, then, is the purpose of the amended law championed by the new Home Minister, Amit Shah, especially if a person branded as a terrorist won't necessarily be convicted or imprisoned?

Manu Sebastian, writing on Livelaw.in gives us a clue: 'An official designation as a terrorist will be akin to "civil death" for a person'; so just about anyone can be at risk of 'social boycott, expulsion from job, hounding by media' and 'can be thrown to the "mob" to suffer extra-judicial punishments'. Well, this too should not matter. Whether individuals can live, speak and think freely and without fear is not the only thing in a democracy.

Back in 1949, George Orwell wrote his great novel *1984*, a vision of the future. I read it in 2019. I come from the same district he was born in—Champaran. But I feel an even greater affinity with him in 2019 because every plot and detail of his novel is a precise reflection of the world we inhabit today. There's a character in the novel whose job is to erase old phrases and slogans from every printed thing. Exactly as many contexts and memories associated with Nehru and Gandhi are being erased in our country. In the novel, there are telescreens everywhere; means by which Big Brother keeps an eye on ordinary citizens. News is broadcast simultaneously from these same screens. This, too is familiar. Our phones and screens are tools of control in ways still unimaginable for many of us. There are at least a few hundred TV channels, all with the same announcements, the same news. This system of supposed news works non-stop to convert citizens into robots.

The Prime Minister may believe that the matter of

whether or not news is published is of no great consequence, but information and its sanctity are central to the idea of a democracy. People may well agree with the PM, but when they are confronted by their own doubts and concerns and look for answers and accountability, they wish for exactly the kind of press that a few of us journalists want to reclaim. It was never perfect. But now it isn't even a shadow of what it was or could have been. This seems all right to many of us; no great tragedy. But when you turn to the press because your pension has been delayed, or your children's school fees are exorbitant, or you are personally a victim of injustice, you find yourself lamenting that the media has sold out.

The shadow of government falls in the newsrooms of TV channels and newspapers. It has been some years since they stopped interrogating the government and holding it accountable. Some of us may still laugh at the kind of questions that are put to our Prime Minister. But a large segment of our population has already begun to see these as the right kind of questions to ask: How do you eat a mango? Do you keep a wallet? What gives you the temperament of a fakir? These were the questions he was asked by a film star in an interview telecast in the middle of the 2019 election campaign in a country with a thousand inequalities to address and a million aspirations to honour and help fulfil. 'How do you eat a mango?' This was accepted as journalism. There was no popular outrage. So it isn't surprising that when journalists are denied access to a government ministry, when citizens' right to information is effectively taken away and a law to make them live in perpetual fear is passed, there are no cries of protest.

Do a simple exercise if you still need to be convinced. Look at the Twitter handles of the most popular news anchors of Indian television and editors with fancy designations. Look at the titles of their shows and editorials. You won't find a single question asked of the government for months together. But every morning and evening they find new virtues in government policies, for which they credit and congratulate the Prime Minister. After a few days, the PM begins to follow these anchors and editors on twitter, and they make a great show of this as evidence of their professional achievement. This isn't all. Other journalists then begin to tweet the PM, pointing out that he hasn't followed them despite similar obedience. So government and media share 'likes' and 'follows'. It's the festive exchange of gifts and candy in our brave new world.

The desire to be followed on Twitter by our popular and all-powerful PM is the greatest professional wish of the stars of Indian journalism. It would be instructive to see what kind of reporting these journalists have done since 2014: What is their record in social activism, or the defence of democracy, or ground-breaking reportage? What exactly is it about their reporting and analysis that makes the PM follow them? But then, our PM also follows abusive trolls, so this isn't surprising. These anchors and editors are trolls, too. They attack and dare the opposition in their programmes. They hunt liberals every evening. They speak the language of hoodlums and bullies.

In newsrooms, no one asks any longer why there is no news in what is put out on the airwaves and in print. The system that relied on reporters has been decimated. Only editors survive. Senior group editor, group editor, senior managing editor, managing editor, national editor, political editor, associate editor. And many other kinds of editors. Now, how can an editor ask another editor, 'Where's the news? Why haven't you given us any news for so long?' All that the newsrooms of scores of channels do is to decide the topics of debates. Many citizens have come to believe this is journalism. And so they say, 'There's been an incident in our neighbourhood, can you arrange a debate about it?' They don't ask for the incident to be covered and reported. People aren't troubled by this. Till the time that they are affected personally, and then they begin to look for the absent reporter. In July 2019, there were strikes in several railway zones. Railway workers joined in the thousands. When the media did not cover the strikes, these workers began to circulate WhatsApp messages of their protests. All the messages said that the media has been bought over.

Up until then these workers were regular and uncritical consumers of anything put out by the same media. Now, when their public protest was blanked out, they began to see that the media had sold out. The truth is, India's mainstream media has reduced the general public to such a state that they end up making videos of their own tragedies and watching these themselves.

I receive phone calls every day from people who say that they, their friends and family prefer watching other channels, not mine, but could I take up their problems in my show? So they know well what is journalism and what isn't. Yet they continue to watch the very channels that they believe don't practice journalism. A large section of the public has been inured to the rotten standards of channels that work overtime to broadcast propaganda instead of news, directing their viewers towards a particular politics, towards one political party.

There was a time when journalists would say that they chose the profession because they did not want just a nine-to-five job. But that is exactly what it has become; in fact, much worse, for it lacks even the rigour and integrity of an honestly done nine-to-five job. Courage and ethics are being banished from the newsroom. Journalists who still have faith in their profession and try to hold on to the old ideals of journalism are being sacked. Their financial security is endangered. If a couple of newspapers or channels somehow find the courage to attempt independent news, the government punishes them by withholding advertisements. It is interesting that even papers that have been punished by the government in this manner don't report the fact. We get the news of their intimidation and taming from the few websites that have emerged as honourable alternatives to the mainstream media. But for these sites, we would not have known of the extraordinary situation when a knife is drawn across someone's neck, like a bow across strings, and he produces music in praise of his assassin.

Was the popular verdict of the 2019 elections also a verdict against the demands for free and fair journalism? There's no conclusive answer to this question yet. But it does appear that the Indian people—certainly a large section of them—did not attach much importance to freedom of the press. For this large section, it is a matter of little consequence that the media sells out or that journalism is dying. In a democracy, governments cannot be judged by the standards of a media that has sold out to authority. But it is being done in India. Our democracy is being hollowed out by the nexus of politics, big business and a compromised media.

Despite all this, I still believe that change will come. Freedom and impartiality of the press may be a dead issue in the corridors of power, but one day it will emerge as a matter of life and livelihood for the general public. For, as long as even a single person feels hunger, as long as anyone feels impelled to speak out, there will be the urge to know the truth. There's dead silence today, but public consciousness will come awake tomorrow. And when it does, people will want to know how India can remain a great democracy if its media is a willing slave to authority and news anchors speak like hired thugs of the establishment.

Why should the preface to a book be written as a news report? When reportage no longer appears where it should, a preface to update a book is a good platform. Prefaces and introductions also escape the notice of people who burn books. But I hope some of them will open this book and read it. It doesn't matter if they agree or disagree with me. I only want them to read it. In fact, I want them to read any book, preferably by someone they oppose.

I'm grateful that a lot of people bought and read the first edition of *The Free Voice*—in English, in Marathi and Kannada. It is now also available in Hindi. This book emerged from a conversation with Ravi Singh. I thank him and everyone else who helped me put it together.

RAVISH KUMAR
New Delhi, July 2019

Speaking Out

'A judge dies. His son and wife are unable to summon up the courage to speak their minds. Shouldn't the Chief Justice of India assure them of safety, making it possible for them to speak? If a citizen, out of fear, loses the courage and the will to live, to speak, who will reassure him? If, as the upholders of the Constitution, the Chief Justice of the Supreme Court and the Prime Minister cannot provide this reassurance, who can? Have we allowed power to become such a blanket of fear that it will keep terrorizing us and we will pull the same blanket over ourselves for security, lying helpless under the very terror that makes us tremble? An ordinary citizen, too, needs answers, or else everyone will believe that if this can happen to a judge, absolutely no one is safe.

I want to confess something to you. I felt fear, too, when I read the story. Yet I'm devoting this Prime Time show to it so that Anuradha Biyani does not feel that her brother, the judge, was probably killed and we did not speak. Judge Loya's son should not feel that someone killed his father and none of his countrymen will speak for him. It isn't as if we aren't afraid; we are. But the way out of this fear was to bring this story before everyone. Now, whatever will be, will be.'

'Now, whatever will be, will be.' This closing sentence of the NDTV India Prime Time Show of 23 November 2017 was for my viewers, and also for myself. I had found release from the fear that had held me in its suffocating grip for two days. Through the duration of the show, I'd felt that every single word was holding me back, as if to warn me: 'Enough, don't go any further. You cannot put yours and yourself in danger just to overcome your fear. Fear does not end after you've spoken out. Even after you've spoken, fear lies in wait for you with its nets and snares.'

But I had spoken, and I was free.

That November afternoon, as I was heading to the NDTV studios to conduct my usual Prime Time show, I was wrestling with the silence surrounding the allegation that a judge had died in suspicious circumstances. The silence lay thick even three days after the news broke. A report had been published in *Caravan* magazine which raised questions about the death of Judge Brijgopal Harkishan Loya, who had been presiding over the CBI court in the

Sohrabuddin Sheikh fake encounter case in Gujarat, in which BJP president Amit Shah was the prime accused. No statement from the judge's wife and son had come after this story broke. Was it because of some terror that the family could not say anything? Can people be so afraid that they cease to have faith in everyone? Even in themselves? I was myself living the fear that must have been inside them. I was worried, too, that the story in *Caravan* could be wrong. I felt as if I had somehow put myself on the line. This story wasn't mine, but now it had become also mine.

I am making no claims about the story in *Caravan*, but the fear and the silence surrounding it had set up a shuddering within me. Perhaps fear is not even the right word for this, but doubt. Doubts create all sorts of restlessness within. They shatter one from the inside; like someone is using a hammer and a chisel to chip away at a wall. Before I broke down and became even more of a ruin, I decided to broadcast Judge Loya's story on prime time.

It was almost 9 p.m. The fear was threatening to overwhelm me. There was no one around me with whom I could share my apprehensions. I looked within myself and saw a news anchor falling into a deep dark well. To save himself, all that he had was his voice, which he wanted to reach to people at maximum pitch and volume. I used each word as the step of a ladder and began to climb out of the depths of my fear. And, after I finished broadcasting the Prime Time episode, it felt as if I had kept a promise which I had made to Judge Loya's wife. I had also freed myself of fear.

But, afterwards, others' fears lay in wait for me. My phone buzzed incessantly. The voices at the other end were all chilled. I felt as if I wouldn't even be able to get home. Unpleasant doubts crept into every conversation. I gradually began to feel alone. It felt as if each person was delivering a final warning before going away. The story in *Caravan* could have been wrong, that was plausible; but other than that apprehension, had I also crossed that line which dictates that certain people and versions of certain stories should not be questioned? Were people actually, genuinely, so afraid of that man at whose doorstep Judge Loya's story finally washed up?

Fear can be real. It can also be imaginary; but the factors which create and control imaginary fears are very real. So speaking out will never be easy. It may even well be an act of bravery, but what is significant is something else. When you speak, you must first challenge yourself. You first become your own interrogator before asking questions of others. If your life is clean and uncorrupted your voice will have the ring of truth. To speak, you must persevere; it isn't a single act done in a moment or without effort. You strain your entire being from within. In the same way in which Usain Bolt leans his body forward into the wind at the finishing line. The farther you lean your body into the finishing line when you speak, the closer you will come to the truth. But the truth is not just a set of bald facts, easily gathered and stated. Truth is also defined by its time, the prevailing environment and the systems that run the institutions in that environment. So while a ribbon awaits Bolt at the finishing line, for people like us, there is a concrete wall. When you reach the finishing line, you run straight into that wall. Everything, your job, your credibility, your life itself, is at stake.

Where your fear ends is where those who sit at the top of the power hierarchy go to work. You are freed from one fear but they will spread ten more around you like booby traps. Courage is nothing but the struggle to emerge from one circle of fear into another, then another; a constant struggle to be free of fear. These days, whenever I write something, say something, afterwards, people introduce me to new and different varieties of fear. Even if what I say is commonplace and non-controversial, people caution me: 'Aren't you afraid? Take care of yourself.' Whenever I hear these words I see a world of fear on the speakers' faces. These exhortations to keep safe have made people cowards. Because they are not warnings to speak carefully, but warnings to not speak at all.

Whenever someone asks me if I am afraid to speak out, fear spreads its wings out within me. I go back to being that Ravish of my boyhood days who would recite the *Hanuman Chalisa* and chant 'Jai Bajrang Bali' as he walked underneath the bel tree. I had heard someone say that ghosts reside in bel trees. If there was no one on the road, I would run as fast as I could, my slippers in my hand. As I ran, my body would become limber and strong and I would forget the ghost; I would even slow down. For the longest time I thought that in later years my fear had vanished because I had left the bel tree behind. I now understand that it was the act of becoming limber and strong which had vanquished the fear. If we do not show mental and physical strength in the face of fear, it will keep us forever standing underneath the bel tree.

This was what used to happen in cinema halls too. As soon as the hall lights would dim, I would become afraid and I would screw my eyes shut during scenes of violence. I have never been able sit through a rape scene in a movie with my eyes open.

At school, the fear of failure would kill me every day during examinations. I was an ordinary student. I had no grasp of science subjects and thus the months of March and April used to be exceedingly sad. My father said to me during one of these moments of fear, 'If you study gradually all year round, you will have no need to cram during examinations. And there will be no need to be terrified either.'

I was leaving home to sit for the mathematics paper during my board examinations. I cried so hard that Babuji had to come along with me. A bucket was filled with water and a rose floated upon its surface, the way in which it is done when a girl leaves her marital home for the first time after marriage. I just wouldn't leave home. I still don't know why Babuji went along with me that day. In the normal course of things he was unbothered with which class I was studying in, which subjects I was bad at and which ones I did well in. As the time came for us to part, I felt like clinging to him and weeping one more time. When he left me at the school gate, Babuji said, 'You shouldn't be so afraid. Why do you have such fear within you? You've prepared well, haven't you?'

I have always remembered Babuji's words. When I came to Delhi and started studying for my graduation, I won over my fear of academic failure. When all my friends would go home to Patna for holidays, I would sit in the library and work on my fear. I made friends with my B.A. examinations.

My mother too remains unfazed by any circumstance. Laughing, she often tells Nayana, 'This one starts crying before anything has even happened. Just the mention of examinations used to be enough to make him cry.' This is the same Nayana because of whom I have become free of fear in all the other areas of my life. But that story is for another telling.

This man whom people ask to be careful and stay safe was a coward for a large part of his life.

I feel a great deal of fear even today. I am very afraid of making mistakes. I make that journey from fear to courage every day. My days start with the trolls' abuses and threats and end with the thought that I should be careful for the sake of my job. Not a day has passed in three years during which I have not heard people talking about the possibility that I might lose my job. But fear is also what saves you from rashness. It is that resting place between courage and rashness. That point from where you commit to a course of action.

Power knows who should be removed from the path of its onward march and when. It maintains a strict calendar and schedule. Despite that, in a democracy, people keep alive the act of speaking out. And the thrill of this journey, between fear and courage, has destroyed my sleep, it has gained me abuse, and sometimes made my ears resound with applause.

One must pay other prices for speaking out too. When colleagues with whom I had worked for twenty years were having to leave the company, many among them looked in my direction. There was a great distance in their eyes. They felt that it was because of me that the government had punished the organization.

During that time I ran into a former colleague in the office bathroom. All he asked was: 'Couldn't we have changed our line of work?' I asked him in return, 'So shouldn't we have become journalists?' My question did not answer his, and I did not have any other answer for him. The experience of losing a job is bitter for everyone, I thought. One should not feel bad or offended by someone's words at such a time. I kept standing before him like time that has already passed. There was no point in expressing the pain that I felt at parting with him. I stood there as upon a shore, inwardly shattered. I do hope that in my colleague's eyes, the men who did not like that a journalist should speak out are as culpable as I am.

'Couldn't we have changed our line of work?'—this statement sank its hooks deep within me. Should I instead have become part of a mob which kills someone on a moving train, which won't allow a movie to be released, which corners a man in his own house and murders him, which climbs on to the roof of a court of justice and unfurls a saffron flag? I thought these thoughts as I walked slowly out of the bathroom. The act of speaking out makes you alone. I have no friends in this profession of mine. Each one I speak to advises me to keep silent.

Even today I feel as if I am tiptoeing underneath the great bel tree of power. The only difference is that I no longer chant the *Hanuman Chalisa*. I don't implore God to preserve my life. Rather, I thank him for all that he has given me. I analyze my facts carefully, I keep my pen straight, and I keep my tongue clean. The ability to speak follows naturally.

My speaking up, and its being viewed within the framework of courage, all of it is thanks to what happened after 2014. Post 2014, the political winds began to change course. Criticism of the government began to be equated with criticism of the nation. A factory called the 'IT Cell' was set up and many varieties of fear were manufactured inside its basement. The trolls of the IT Cell mounted fierce attacks on anyone who dared to ask questions. They were called many things, from anti-nation and anti-religion to even pimps of the opposition parties. Many journalists were cast in the mould of an opposition. They were called anti-Modi. Even serving ministers began to attack reporters. The IT Cell rapidly transformed media into 'godi media'—lapdog media. Many anchors and journalists crept into the laps of power and began chanting the *Modi Chalisa.*

The IT Cell is not simply the unit of a particular party. It is a mentality which has formed among a large section of society. I call that entire set, the collective of people who share that mentality, the 'IT Cell'. This IT Cell has transformed a large section of the citizenry into trolls. Many people find this idea of the mentality of the IT Cell a joke, but this is a fully realized human resource which works extensively from the metropolises to far-flung areas of India. Many of the news channels which work in today's India are an extension of this IT Cell.

This IT Cell has its own laboratory: the WhatsApp University. The amount of history that this WhatsApp University has tried to teach in three years would not have been taught in the seventy years since Independence by all historians together. The only difference is that the history taught in the WhatsApp University is fake and poisonous. Even India's first prime minister, Jawaharlal

Nehru, fell victim to this WhatsApp University. His clan, his religion and his name were all changed and distorted. He became a greater 'villain' than Jinnah, than whom there is no man more evil for the IT Cell and its parent family. Gandhi has not been spared either; in this case the IT Cell laboratory does what certain politicians cannot afford to do in public, though they privately wish Gandhi had never existed.

The WhatsApp University has also extensively defamed, vilified and abused journalists like Rajdeep Sardesai, Rana Ayyub, Sagarika Ghose, Barkha Dutt and me, among others. The handful of us journalists, who are only doing our job, have been declared traitors. We have been blamed for every injustice committed in India. A new benchmark has been set up in the WhatsApp University as far as speaking out is concerned: 'Why didn't you speak then, and why are you speaking only now?' With this mischievous statement, the public has been handed a weapon. People have been told, 'Any time they ask a question, ask them, "Where were you when *that* happened?"'

I remained enmeshed among these questions for a long time. I kept thinking, 'I am a journalist, I am not myself a newspaper. I cannot comment on everything. And keeping quiet doesn't mean that I become a party to injustices.' Why didn't you speak then?—this is a design by which a sense of guilt is created within that person who asks questions. And those who ask that artful question conveniently forget to ask those who remain silent why they aren't speaking.

Since 2014, I have found myself dealing and arguing, not with the government, but with the new armies it has built in our society. The generation that has emerged from the WhatsApp University has become the private army shielding the government and it demands the name and address of anyone who is critical of the government. Soon they'll be asking us for our Aadhar numbers before deciding whether we can ask the Modi government any questions or not. A mob has been created which will harass and intimidate us on behalf of Power. This mob is answerable to no one, as long it remains a cheerleader for the establishment. When we demand accountability from the government, the mob is let loose.

This mob broadcasts new rumours and lies every day. These lies don't disappear into a void. I've seen them seep into lakhs, if not crores, of minds. The establishment has outsourced its power to this tireless mob which will surround one anywhere, at any time. Every day I'm stalked by a new lie. Every day I fight a new lie. It would be exhausting, but for the occasional sign that the fight is not in vain.

In January 2018 I was doing a series for Prime Time on jobs in the country. The government institutions that recruit people take an average of four years to fill a single vacancy, when there are millions seeking jobs—and there are very few vacancies to begin with. After one of the first programmes in the series, a young man called Rahul phoned me from Bihar's Aara town. I had met him when I was in Bihar in 2015, covering the high-voltage Assembly elections. He was calling me now, over two years after that meeting, he said, because he wanted to apologize. He said I had spoken about young people like him in my series on jobs, no one else had bothered, and this when he and many of his friends had abused and hated me for long. He said local members of the Bajrang Dal had convinced them I was anti-Hindu and anti-Modi. I was anti-India. I was a Communist and my annual salary package was one crore plus perks. That would have made me a very rare Indian Communist indeed. Rahul went on to say that he had also been taught to hate Muslims and had his head filled with the poison of communalism. He had wasted his life. He was purging himself of the poison.

It's this poison of hate that I'm fighting, too. It has spread all around me. It has ruined many young minds. These young men wander about with explosive hatred inside them. They want to find a way out of the hell they have been pushed into. But there's hardly anyone around to help them climb out. On good days, I feel I can be the one to help.

It's one of the things that keeps me focused, despite the torrent of abuse I face even when I write about something as neutral as the weather. These aren't routine abuses used by people. These are rocks and stones hurled by Power that fall all around and create a wall of mental despondency. Enduring these abuses has begun to feel like an exercise in sensing the true heft of Power.

Abuse is a part of the culture of India. Abuses are exchanged during marriages; there is societal sanction for abuse in some relationships. But never before today has abuse been a weapon at the hands of Power. When the mob which stands in support of Power hurls abuse, it becomes so much more. That mob wants to terrify you. This, then, is the decision you must make: do you want to be terrified? Even when an entire system exists, complete with abuse, and when there is no one to stand with you?

What I cannot understand is: what is it that one is doing that is so wrong? Why is it that for asking a few questions, one should be punished so severely that a mob is set loose after one? I have been at the receiving end of people's anger in many places. Men have chased me sometimes, sticks in hand; at others, people have grabbed me by the collar. There have even been incidents of pushing and shoving. I have grown more and more alone in the course of this process. I started speaking out to combat my loneliness. That was the only act which would shatter my isolation.

Each of these acts has made me less and less wanted in my profession. It has become normal in all conversations about journalism with friends for them to tell me that I will lose my job before anyone else and I won't find employment anywhere else either. As the advice about doors slamming shut—in the professional space, upon life itself—has poured in, speaking out is the only window that I have sought through which air and light—though they may be in limited quantities—stream in.

In 2015, Aamir Khan expressed his concern, though in a muted fashion, about the climate of insecurity he and his family felt in India and he was instantly attacked by the IT Cell mob. That same mob remained silent at the Karni Sena's call to Kshatriya personnel in the army to stop eating in their messes to protest against the release of the film *Padmavati*. One man openly talked about instigating communal rebellion within the army and the entire government stood before that man, heads bowed in supplication.

The mob has established a government of fear. It can scare Aamir Khan, claiming to be acting for others, because he practices a religion different from the one practiced by the mob. If it wants, that mob can strike fear into the heart of Sanjay Leela Bhansali too, who is of the same religion. There is just one law in operation, the law of fear.

Every mob is based upon the foundation of fear. Responding to external fears, many people started becoming part of the mob. These individuals first feared their own fellow citizens because of their religion; then, once they joined the mob, they learnt fear from the masters and controllers of the mob. The reason for their silence was simple. They understood, 'If the mob can do this to these people, it can do the same to me.' People joined the mob to silence others; what they did not realize was that they had also learnt to become and remain silent.

On social media too, people have stopped speaking out because of the terror of the IT Cell. Women, especially, have stopped commenting on political matters in large numbers. They don't express their opinion in the 'comments' section but do so in messages sent to inboxes. Not just women, many other people now do the same.

When I set up my page on Facebook, @RavishKaPage, many women inboxed me to say that after having commented on my posts, they were trolled by people who would tell them the different ways in which they would be defamed and assaulted. Frequently, there are a thousand comments on my posts but the women among them don't number even one hundred. The abuses which depend upon Power to propel themselves work like bullets. Everyone is afraid of bullets. Even many boys have told me that they have been forbidden to comment on my page by their parents. The socialization of fear is complete. To be afraid is to be civilized in this new, enfeebled democracy. But I find it uncivilized and impolitic. It is an impoliticness that is inflicted upon democracy.

The IT Cell has accomplished the task of laying down fear with ferocious detail and efficiency. The language of the IT Cell has become the language of the ministers of the government as well as that of the supporters of the government. It was the government which used to strike fear into the hearts of citizens; now the mainstream media and social media are its active allies.

My phone number is frequently made public on Facebook and WhatsApp. The language of provocation that accompanies the act of making my number public should be part of a special study. Sentences are written in such a clever manner that on reading, it isn't clear if a death threat is being issued or if it is being ordered that I should be verbally abused. 'This is the number of the Pakistani Ravish Kumar, please call him and give him a lesson in nationalism.' The posts are in this tenor. All of this is enough to scare a man. The good thing was that as soon as my number was made public, some people became exceedingly happy. They called to say where they had got the number from, but also clarified that they weren't trolls but fans. These same people also later sent me screenshots of those pages which expressed hate.

We seem to living in a climate of fear and suspicion. 'Hang on, not over the phone. I'll call on WhatsApp.' Talk to any official and you will find that he thinks that some minister is getting his phone tapped. Ministers think that their seniors are recording their calls. Journalists feel that their conversations are being listened to. In every other conversation, reporters mention phone tapping. No one has proof of these things, but everyone fears that their calls are being recorded. This fear is so pervasive that it makes even routine meetings suspicious. The suspicion engendered by fear has cast a deep effect on meetings and on the act of speaking.

Ask yourself: Has speaking out become fraught with risk? Does speaking about the government make you afraid? Who are you scared of: the government or of that mob present around you in different avatars? Do you speak out up to a point and stop, or do you continue and finish whatever it is that you wanted to say? Do you seek a society in which people crawl around terrified of the government and some mob for no reason, and only those who sing praises of the government night and day strut with their chests puffed out? And why is it that those who criticize the government should be faced with fears and doubts? Only because there is no faith left in institutions, is it not? Who knows which case one will be embroiled in, and then one will be forced to make the rounds of the courts for years. This is very easily done in India.

In Delhi, which is the centre of India's power politics, the effect of suspicions and doubts has changed the way in which people have conversations. Some refrain from making photographs public on Facebook, while others don't communicate on WhatsApp so that texts can't be used as evidence. Whenever I meet people I come away with yet one more new code word whose only purpose is that the government should not find out in case it tries to snoop. This statement is becoming ever more common: 'We should not talk about this on the phone.' If politics transforms society to such an extent that it calls the dissenter a traitor, putting a barbed wire of intimidation between itself and citizens, then that is a form of violence too.

For those people in Delhi who are connected with governmental work, for those who assess and analyze the work of the government, cellphones—even the most expensive models—have become a source of great insecurity. They carry their phones upon their person but have no faith in them. Things have reached such a pass that when politicians from the ruling party call, the word 'unknown' flashes on the screen. Politicians, too, are very alert that no word of criticism should roll off their tongues.

'That finger which is raised against him, that hand which is raised against him; we will come together to break that hand or, if necessary, to hack it off.'

These words emerged from the mouth of Nityanand Rai, the secretary of the Bihar unit of the BJP and a Member of Parliament, because it has now become normal to strike fear into people's hearts. This is not the first statement of its kind in Indian politics. Nor is it the last. We will hear more of its kind in the future. All you can do is to don metal armour on your fingers—and on your neck because matters have now gone upwards, from cutting off fingers to hacking at necks.

During the controversy surrounding the release of the film *Padmavati*, now *Padmavat*, an official of the Haryana unit of the BJP, Surajpal, announced a reward of ten crore rupees to anyone who would bring him the heads of Deepika Padukone and Sanjay Leela Bhansali. A man from Meerut had earlier declared a reward of five crores, which Surajpal upped to ten, as if upgrading someone from economy class to business. In that same Meerut, in 2006, Yakub Qureishi of the Bahujan Samaj Party had announced a reward of eleven crores, which some media reports pegged at fifty-one crores, for the head of a cartoonist from Denmark. (I do hope there isn't a bank in Meerut which gives out loans on EMIs for cutting off heads!) Back then such criminality was still abnormal. Now it is routine. On 12 April 2017, a politician from the BJP Yuva Morcha, Yogesh Varshney, declared that whoever brought him the head of the West Bengal chief minister Mamata Banerjee would be given eleven lakh rupees. It is a sign of the times that the amount sounds paltry. Could it be that the demonetization of November 2016 had an effect? Perhaps the man had run out of cash.

If you think that the threat to cut off a hand in response to speaking against the Prime Minister is an uncommon one, you should pay attention to one more statistic which I have collected from Google. Between 2014 and November 2017, more than forty people were either arrested or had cases slapped against them for criticizing Prime Minister Modi and UP chief minister Yogi Adityanath or sharing posts about them.

It isn't easy to speak out against Power. Before you speak, you will have to choose between jail and amputation. Or a lynching. For mobs have no fear of the law.

There are many different kinds of mobs: One mob might set out on the issue of cow slaughter; another on the equally spurious issue of love jihad; yet another because a certain film was made. The social structures of different mobs are distinct in themselves, but they all have one thing in common: the cloak of religious fervor. The fear of these mobs is silencing many a young person who wants to speak about politics but is now staying away from Facebook altogether. This is how an atmosphere of silence is created. You don't speak when you should.

The social sanction for speaking out is lessening. This isn't happening only because of the fear of governments or the mob but also because devotion to religion has been strongly established in a large section of the citizenry. That devotion prepares the ground for the majority to remain silent. And because of that devotion, they are comfortable with the joke that is being made out of democracy in the name of their religion. More precisely, given the behavior and discourse of the present dispensation, one should call this devotion to the Hindu religion. The unfortunate thing is that this devotion is not born out of Hinduism's capacious and generous traditions but out of the fear of a handful of goonda organizations. That citizen who is laid siege to by the fear generated by these organizations might believe himself to be, at least on paper, loyal to the Constitution, but his behaviour is contrary to everything that the Constitution stands for.

If Indian democracy is to be modernized, it is vital that devotion to the Constitution of the land be widely promoted. Blind devotion to any religion will always run down and deem inferior this devotion to the Constitution. Which is why, when the secretary of the Shri Rajput Karni Sena, Mahipal Singh Makrana, called out for the Kshatriya soldiers of the Indian Army to boycott food in their messes to protest against the film *Padmavati*, the common man did not understand what that implied and none of the political parties had the courage to unreservedly denounce this call. The Rajputs protesting the film could have registered their protest using Constitutional means. Instead, they were out on the streets, unleashing violence. What emboldened some of them so much that they could stone a bus full of school children? Why did the government and the opposition not unite to condemn them and ensure action against them? Why was there no public outcry? The majority population did not demand action. Was their devotion to Hinduism stopping them? Would they have stayed silent if people of a different faith had stoned a school bus? How has a shared religious identity come to mean this?

It is this blind religiosity that gives licence to the mob. The mob is greater even than the Constitution.

A powerful fear is created over maniacal debates on TV channels. Many news anchors swarm like fearsome attackers all over those who ask questions. The common viewer of TV channels sees this and starts losing confidence. He can see what becomes of those who raise questions. He feels that there is danger in standing apart from the mob. So he stays quiet, and by his silence he becomes a part of the mob. Fear has seeped into people's consciousness.

This has had the greatest effect on the minority community. It has begun to keep out of every kind of debate. And the space which has been vacated by the community has been filled up by those maulanas, who do represent Muslims, but speak like those very majority institutions in whose communal agendas these maulanas are caught up. These maulanas have made Muslims even more insecure. To the extent that Muslim friends advise me that I should avoid platforms where issues related to their community are being debated. So this is the extent to which they have been made to feel politically irrelevant. Most Muslims now feel that if they were to take to the streets with their demands, the media will see only their beards or their sherwanis, and it will not talk about their issues. This is what the acceptance of one's status as a second-class citizen means.

The status of second-class citizenry has fallen not just to the minority community, but also to people from the majority community. In this democracy of fear, religion is not the only determinant of minority status; the act of questioning the government too can transform you into a minority.

'Ravish-ji, aren't you afraid of speaking out?' 'How do you speak out in such an atmosphere?' 'Doesn't your family forbid you?' I have no substantial answers to these questions. What is it I am saying, after all, that I should be specially praised for it? I am only expressing the views of the people. Why should anyone feel that I possess an ore of courage within me which people can mine by repeatedly asking me how I do my job? Are people afraid?

Everyone who asks me these questions feels that Ravish will give a fitting reply: he will say that he drinks a glass of Bournvita before leaving home. Or that he offers a laddoo to Hanuman. I have no magical mantra as far as the act of speaking out is concerned. I know that Power will make my life such hell that it will be difficult for me to survive in my profession. There are many Hindi-language newspapers already which do not accept my articles. Before 2014, I would be irritated by constant phone calls from these same newspapers asking me to write for them.

What I say isn't very brave in itself. Those who hear what I have to say are so terrified that my speaking out at all seems courageous. They ask how it is that I speak when they are rendered mute by fear. There are many who joke that Bihari people feel no fear. Which Bihari would not feel chuffed hearing good words about his home? But this is not a question about being Bihari. Marathis speak out, Bengalis do. Gujaratis speak out, too. And those who speak out in Gujarat have heard and seen much worse. I am not the only one doing the talking. Many other journalists are writing too. But now newspapers in their respective languages don't publish what they write.

To speak out is not difficult. What is hard is to walk through the tunnel of fear before the act of talking. That fear is not always the fear of Power. One is scared of making mistakes. The fear of possible reactions to what one has to say also bothers one. The battle with fear begins once you have said what you wanted to. It is then you understand whether you have the courage to face that which you have said: when friends call, exhorting you to stay alert. To stay quiet. That times are bad. There might be just one call out of ten in which the caller might say, 'It doesn't matter. Don't worry. Keep speaking.' Most of the rest have faith neither in the institutions of the land nor in society. And everyone feels that the world doesn't care at all.

Advice given by friends and family also creates fear within you. I was giving a speech at the Press Club after Gauri Lankesh was murdered. Many of the people present there were looking at me as they might have looked at Gauri. Their eyes were filled with a sense of warning. They put their hands on my shoulder as they left, as if to tell me, 'You're next.' They were loading their fears on to me. Many viewers called me after they saw my speech at the Press Club. For a few days I kept walking about like a living corpse. Messages were arriving in my mobile phone inbox urging me to take care of myself. Get some security, they said, at least register an FIR with the police. Viewers who were watching me were very stressed. The IT Cell had performed its task of striking fear well.

That you live amidst such well-meaning advice is enough. In today's time, we are giving our fears away to others. People are sharing their fears by becoming supporters of the government too. I frequently meet people who tell me, 'Stop digging around Modi-ji's foundations. Reform yourself.' Is all this fear which surrounds us because of Modi-ji? Really? Will it go away if we stop being critical of Modi-ji? I don't think so. The jinn is out of the bottle.

And what am I writing, or broadcasting in my programmes, that a supporter of the government should fear that some game of the establishment will be disrupted? I, at least, harbour no such illusion. All the rules which once governed the media are destroyed, after all. Ninety per cent of the media is filled with praise. Wherever there are critics, they are being attacked. They are called upon to be more than impartial. But those who break all rules of journalism to play in the lap of power know no definition of impartiality.

Just as an individual seeks a way to free himself from fear, an alive and conscious society wages war to emerge from its fears. If you live in fear of being killed, you aren't really alive, even though you may be physically so. You can be sure that you are alive only when you speak out. He who cannot, misses out in life. So everyone should speak. It is very important also that we begin teaching our children to speak up and to speak out right from a young age and at home. Don't stop them. We keep forbidding our children at home and, one day, the fear they feel spreads out of the home and into the world. Most of our fears are created and sustained in our homes, where we are taught to keep silent.

Ask yourself one question: Are you afraid of speaking out, of criticizing authority? Why are you afraid? Do you choose a system only to inflict fear upon yourself? Are you afraid of being killed or being isolated, of being alone? If you aren't fearful of being killed, then also banish the fear that you will fall alone among your friends. You can risk at least this much. If you have friends whose devotion is to something you think to be wrong, tell them that. If you cannot speak up before friends, how will you ever stand before the government to criticize it? You will have to start practicing speaking up somewhere. Things aren't so bad yet that no one can speak out.

If you are afraid of criticizing Prime Minister Modi, say whatever you want against the first prime minister, Nehru. What you say will not affect Nehru in any way and you will learn to stand before an institution such as the prime minister and ask questions. Just make sure that your questions are correct when you do ask them. Check your facts. Don't allow hatred towards the person to seep into your questions. He who is in the dominating position of power decides the rules of morality. He might himself be immoral, but will request you to stick to principles of ethics and morality. That, too, is one of the conditions of speaking out, so keep gathering maximum points on morality. Stick to ethics at all times. Keep your life clean and uncluttered. And keep speaking out.

The Robo-Public and the Building of a New Democracy

Voting in the two-phase Gujarat elections of 2017 had just begun. Reports from the ground suggested that the BJP, after more than twenty years in power, was losing the support of large sections of the Gujarati public, and that this could benefit the opposition Congress. Prime Minister Narendra Modi had been campaigning extensively across his home state, and now he arrived in Palanpur to address a large crowd. Somewhere in the middle of his speech, which was widely quoted in the media, he said:

> *There was a meeting of the high commissioner of Pakistan, the former foreign minister of Pakistan, the former vice president of India and the former prime minister of India Manmohan Singh at Mani Shankar Aiyar's house... The next day, Mani Shankar Aiyar said Modi is "neech"... My brothers and my sisters, this is a grave matter. Pakistan is a sensitive issue; what was the reason behind this secret meeting with that high commissioner, especially when elections are taking place in Gujarat? And another thing: the former director general of the Pakistani army*

Arshad Rafiq said that the election of Ahmed Patel as the chief minister of Gujarat should be supported.

This statement made by Narendra Modi on 9 December 2017 is a classic example of fake news. It should be taught in mass communication classrooms. Only one fact in this statement is strictly true—that some people had gathered in the Congress leader Mani Shankar Aiyar's house in New Delhi. All the other facts are either incomplete or false. No secret meeting had been organized; it was a dinner gathering, for which invitations had been sent by regular email to several people, including journalists. The Prime Minister correctly identified, by name, some of the people who were at the dinner but he did not read out the full list of the guests. He was well aware of what we learned later, from reports published by some newspapers the day after his statement: India's former chief of army staff, Deepak Kapoor, was also present at the dinner, along with a former foreign secretary and other senior Indian diplomats whose integrity is unquestionable. All of them said to the media that there had been no discussion on Gujarat at all, but after the Prime Minister had said what he had to say, the dinner was discussed all over Gujarat.

Barring one or two, none of the mainstream media institutions checked the veracity of the Prime Minister's statement. Most of them simply quoted him verbatim. Sample some of the headlines which were published by newspapers and news websites on 10 December 2017:

> *Gujarat polls: Why Pakistan army ex-DG wants Ahmed Patel as CM, asks Narendra Modi [Mint on Sunday]*
>
> *Narendra Modi alleges Pakistan is interfering in Gujarat assembly polls; Seeks explanation from Congress over its top party members meeting leaders from Pakistan [Mid-Day]*
>
> *Narendra Modi accuses Pakistan of interfering in Gujarat polls, claims it wants Ahmed Patel as chief minister [FirstPost]*
>
> *Pakistan trying to influence Gujarat polls, claims PM Narendra Modi at Palanpur rally [New Indian Express]*

Using the Prime Minister's statement as a firm base, the media then played an even bigger game with the headlines. Though the Prime Minister was wrong in what he had said, the fact that he was wrong, that he had twisted facts, was not discussed or even mentioned. The Prime Minister is a past master of insinuation and innuendo. He is always innocent, he lights no fires himself. In this case, he gave the cue and the media, like a mob plugged into a single brain, obliged by constructing the narrative he desired. All he did in Palanpur was to inform the people of a 'secret meeting', draw their attention to the timing of the meeting, and then add that a retired officer of the Pakistan army wanted a Congressman with a Muslim name to become chief minister of Gujarat. He did not explicitly say anything. He did not need to. The obliging media went to town with headlines saying that according to the country's prime minister, Pakistan was interfering in the elections underway in Gujarat, and the Congress was colluding with it. Once the idea of interference had been planted, the BJP gave it utmost veracity by using it to attack the Congress every time it questioned the BJP's claims about development in Gujarat. The regular consumer of news would have felt that there surely must be something to what the Prime Minister had said, or his party would not be so vociferous.

It is this factor—'there must be something'—which serves as fuel for fake news. When the Congress party demanded that the Prime Minister apologize for his lie, Finance Minister Arun Jaitley responded belligerently, wanting to know why the party was asking for an apology when it should be divulging the details of the 'secret meeting' to the citizens of India.

The situation changed completely after the elections were over and the BJP had scraped through in Gujarat.

When the proceedings of the Rajya Sabha—where the BJP doesn't yet have a majority—were interrupted by the Congress protesting against the Prime Minister's remarks and insisting that he apologize, Arun Jaitley issued an apology disguised as an explanation:

> *PM in his speeches didn't question, nor meant to question the commitment to this nation of either former PM Manmohan Singh or Former VP Hamid Ansari. Any such perception is erroneous; we hold these leaders in high esteem, as well as their commitment to India.*

There was no mention of the 'secret meeting'. It was as if the Prime Minister had never whipped up a storm over a spurious issue to fool citizens and, in the process, all but accused a former prime minister of India, a former vice president and a former chief of the Indian army of treason.

Read every word of the statement made by Arun Jaitley and what the Prime Minister said during the Gujarat elections, and you will find that fake news is not merely an electoral game but a phenomenon for which statements are crafted with a great deal of intelligence and very strategically. Images are created and so are impressions, all for a specific, ugly purpose.

The manufacturing of fake news is a high-skilled game.

It seems simple, but is based on a deep knowledge of the psychology of the common man. Most items of fake news are connected with issues about which people have partial information—more impressions than facts. For instance, there are many impressions about the Partition of India in the minds of people, especially now that very few of those who actually experienced it are alive. Fake news or posts connected with Partition are concocted based upon these unverifiable impressions of the event. So a continuity of false impressions exists and, because of that, no one doubts the veracity of the fake news. In the matter of the 'secret meeting' at Mani Shankar Aiyar's house, too, a continuity existed. The sharp and controversial statements he had made about Narendra Modi and the BJP in the past and his consistent championing of peace talks with Pakistan were enough to present him and his party as permanent villains.

Thus, for me, more important than the Prime Minister's statement and the clarification offered by Jaitley a few weeks later is the psychological process of the formation and dissemination of fake news. Each word of those statements was a classic example of the construction of an untruth. And if fake news comes from the Prime Minister himself, it soon becomes almost the genuine article and travels quickly to and among the masses. All of politics, then, becomes fake.

There is research which tries to show that fake news has no impact upon democracy; but it does, which is why the Prime Minister's 'secret meeting' speech remained hotly discussed throughout the elections in Gujarat. After Arun Jaitley delivered that apology-disguised-as-explanation in the Rajya Sabha afterwards, unwittingly implying but never admitting that the Prime Minister had misled people, there was no way left for citizens to hold the BJP and its leaders accountable for what was, essentially, a lie constructed to manipulate them. It is possible that many residents of Gujarat still bear the burden of impressions that were formed after hearing the falsity peddled to them. And if nothing else, the Prime Minister succeeded in wiping out other, genuine and concrete issues from the public consciousness for at least some time.

Fake news engenders fake debates, and fake debates result in fake politics. It is a means to take the focus far away from the real problems that affect people. Citizens keep wandering around, looking to have their problems addressed, and political leaders hand them fake news and conspiracy theories and make a mockery of their lives. This is not a phenomenon that is created only during elections; rather, it is an entire process, a strategy to keep adding many obfuscating layers to just about everything. You emerge from one lie or half-truth only to be entangled in another. To fight fake news means to wage a struggle against oneself and to work very hard for information at all times. Very few manage to do this.

Fake news is a tool that Power uses to transport citizens to an alternative reality where, forgetting their real and urgent problems, they find themselves confronted by manufactured worries of a national scale. Citizens who allow themselves to be manipulated in this manner do the greatest harm to themselves, complicit in their own material, intellectual and moral impoverishment. A people cut off from reality can also be extremely dangerous. They become a mob which, with the aid of some major piece of false information, can be primed to commit violence.

Today, most media platforms speak the same language. The society which falls within the ambit of their influence is left with very limited options to seek facts. On almost every news channel, in every programme, false realities are being created on the basis of spurious issues and counterfeit agendas driven by the government and big business. This happens on a daily basis. Power has shifted reality with the aid of the media. For instance, communalism has already been covered with the garb of nationalism. The media has now begun to present communal attitudes as valid, legitimizing them as nationalism. Since viewers and readers have limited options for gleaning information, they are forced into the public consensus manufactured by the government—by the government's PR machinery and the corporate media (there is now little to distinguish the two). It is not easy to escape this web of images and misinformation, and very few actually do.

Truth is the only thing that citizens have with which to challenge authority—the truth which springs from the conditions of their everyday life. So Power erects the wall of an imaginary reality before the genuine realities of a people. Power in India today recognizes the fact that conditions of life cannot change rapidly; nor does it really have the wherewithal to change them. So an instrument is needed, one which will constantly provide an 'alternative condition' to the people. Fake news is the foundational basis of the process of continually creating alternative conditions. It carries on relentlessly.

Fake news, fake debate is not only an alternative to news, it is also the means by which an alternative *citizenry* is being created—a gathering of people who are fed false information and polarizing impressions that amplify and legitimize their prejudices. These people are freed from the burden of thinking for themselves; they become like a mob and their political behaviour like that of a robot. I call this the 'robo-public'. Those who comprise the robo-public cannot be changed by any argument. All you can do, in desperation or in anger, is to label them as blinkered foot soldiers, as 'bhakts'. The robo-public is used to living in alternative conditions which have nothing to do with reality. It has been programmed through a gradual robotification that involves appealing to its emotions rather than to reason—in fact, the spreading of false information is done without pause and always with maximum noise so that there remains no possibility of nuance and reason. Fake news is the coded language which can be used to control and use the robo-public.

The people who make up a genuine democracy are not an inert, lifeless unit. They constantly pulse and transform on the basis of information. Consider a scenario in which all the various pathways of information are controlled and, through them, only one kind of information is disseminated—false information which cannot be questioned. What kind of a citizenry will be created? The question is not what will happen to that citizenry at the end of a decade or two of such control, the question is what kind of a people will that citizenry be *during* those ten or twenty years. People who see no alternatives in the information they receive stop seeing alternatives in politics, too. So what kind of democracy will a robo-public make up?

I have seen many people who behave like robots. They dismiss every kind, every manner of argument. They use the very impressions on the basis of which they are programmed to dismiss not only contrary opinion, but also discussion. They listen to nothing, they read nothing, they only see the one face they have been programmed to see. Those who behold a different sight are enemies and traitors—in the context of India, they would be anti-Modi, anti-Hindu, anti-national. They aren't few, these robots, they exist in sufficient numbers to take over every debate and create an atmosphere of fear in society through their aggressive reactions. We have no way of dealing with them. In combating the robo-public, personal relations within families change; we stop speaking out, overcome by fatigue. We cannot sit with robots and have a conversation; we cannot look at the moon and the stars with them and wonder at the great mysteries of the universe; we cannot comfort them and they cannot comfort us.

The most extreme robots are the bhakts. No serious research has been conducted to see how, in politics, bhakts are constructed out of supporters. Most people take this process lightly and believe that bhakts are a temporary phenomenon, that this is a trend which—like every other trend—will fade away with time. Some bhakts will indeed change with time, but they will be very few in number. The robo-public, the potential bhakts, aren't so few that they can be written off or ignored. It is a particular ideology which programmes them, and the scale of this operation is enormous. New issues are created and ever more fake news and rage are generated constantly on the basis of an exclusivist ideology, so that the number of robots multiplies and they always remain in robot mode—forever demonstrating their faith in the ideology which is now their sole identity.

To keep up the impression of a mob that surrounds you everywhere and at all times is the chief task of the bhakts. Many people who don't wish to join the ranks of the robo-public stop writing and speaking out of fear of this mob. But not everyone likes being silenced; there are some who do manage to overcome this fear and speak out, even taking up cudgels against fake news. So the robo-public is being programmed yet again—to brand these remarkable people who unmask untruth as purveyors of 'fake news' themselves! This is the final treachery of the ideology that creates the robo-public. What can be a greater negation of humanity, of life and existence itself, than the erasing of difference between truth and falsehood, between right and wrong?

Fake news first falsified news and journalism and it is now turning the citizens fake. The robo-public is a fake public. A fake public makes a fake republic, a fake political consciousness, a fake democracy.

The WhatsApp University is the biggest laboratory for fake news. In this laboratory, the process of vilifying anyone who stands in opposition to the bhakts of the present regime goes on constantly so that the robo-public does not have a chance to shift its loyalties. All the possibilities of alternative viewpoints are run down and made invalid. In this university, your photograph will be taken and made suspicious, it will be circled in red and made to go viral. You will be presented as a criminal to society.

I was covering the Delhi chief minister Arvind Kejriwal's roadshow in Patiala during the Punjab elections of 2017. I and my cameraman colleague were travelling in the same open jeep as Arvind Kejriwal—he was standing towards the front of it. A photographer positioned on a rooftop gestured to me, asking that I get the chief minister to look up so that he could take a photograph. I did, and the photographer got his picture. This photograph was made to go extensively viral, with the caption that I was an agent working for Arvind Kejriwal and was helping him in his campaign. The photographer contacted me on WhatsApp many days later. He thanked me and said that though I had been badmouthed, he received many 'hits' on the photograph he had taken. The misrepresentation had made him popular. Perhaps it had furthered his career.

A small example, but I hope it will help you better understand PM Modi's speech in Palanpur during the Gujarat elections. And when you think about this, remember why you elect prime ministers. Remember that you entrust them with the nation and everything that gives it dignity and stature. You trust them.

Across the world, fake news has become the preferred way to subvert democracy and for authoritarian regimes to do as they please. From the capital cities to far-flung districts, an elaborate infrastructure has been developed to manufacture and spread fake news. Governments and their favoured corporations do this in tandem. Statements of heads of state carrying misleading information are printed on the front pages and flashed on prime-time television and when the misrepresentation is pointed out, none of these papers or channels summon the courage or even have the will to report that the prime minister or president has lied. In March 2017, Reporters without Borders released a report which rated countries across the world on the basis of the freedom of the press—India was ranked 136 among 180 countries. The performance of any government should be evaluated, along with everything else, on the grounds of whether the media is free during its tenure—and it isn't just overt censorship that is a threat to press freedom but also the phenomenon of 'godi media'—the lapdog media which functions as the PR department of the government. A UN committee warned in a statement on 4 March 2017 that across the world, people occupying constitutional positions are either declaring independent media organizations liars or calling them the opposition. Fake news is being used to impose a new kind of censorship. Critical thought is being suppressed.

In March 2017, the Democrats, who are in the opposition in America, proposed a bill which said that matters have reached such a stage that fake news is being fed to American citizens by the President himself, and by his spokespersons. Governments, organizations and universities all over the world are discussing fake news. It is a big problem in the Philippines. The president of the country, Rodrigo Duterte, has been accused of encouraging fake news to keep his hold on power. A Filipino senator has filed a bill in the senate which seeks to impose heavy penalties on government officials and media persons who spread fake news, including imprisonment ranging from five to twenty years.

In November 2016, the University of Philippines launched an online channel, TVUP, to combat fake news. The executive director of the university issued a statement saying that he hoped that through this channel, the trash that was strewn in the online space could be countered so that the citizens of that country would have the opportunity to read genuine articles and access genuine news. The Sports Media and Cultural Committee of the British Parliament has also initiated an investigation of the effect of fake news on democracy.

On the other hand, politicians and the agencies of political parties who broadcast fake news have begun a new campaign. The president of the US, Donald Trump, has accused the news channel CNN of spreading fake news. He does that to whichever media criticizes his government. The president of Turkey, Recep Erdogan, sent many journalists to jail claiming that by doing so he was combating the spread of fake news. The prime minister of Cambodia branded the media as anarchist, and said the foreign media working in the country was a threat to peace and stability. The Supreme Court of Cambodia even dismantled the country's principal opposition party. The current age of media and Power is rife with many such examples.

In India, some websites are battling fake news at their own levels. Between 2014 and 2017, many kinds and episodes of fake news were used to stoke tensions in society. The migration of families out of Kairana village in the Saharanpur district of UP in 2015-16 was given a communal colour by the BJP and its affiliates and debates continuously raged on TV that Kairana had been transformed into another Kashmir, with Hindus there being forced to flee 'Muslim terror' like the Kashmiri Pandits. This was a dangerous game in which prominent newspapers and news channels participated. The websites altnews.in, indiaspend.com, boomlive.com, www.hoax-slayer.net and—in Hindi—the website mediavigil.com have started to take up arms against such fake news. Pratik Sinha of altnews.in has managed to take the veils off fake news generated by numerous ministers, governments and websites. But this is happening on a very small scale. These valiant efforts make a very small dent on the fake news spread by the vast majority of the mainstream media.

It is imperative that we define fake news very clearly. The common man hasn't yet understood the many ways in which it is disseminated. Mistakes are committed in journalism, and every mistake isn't fake news. But the specially crafted fake news that emerges regularly these days originates elsewhere and is fed to journalists and media houses, who reach it to everyone. People occupying constitutional positions then legitimize it with their statements. There is also another way in which fake news is being generated: all governments are stopping information from reaching the media. No one possesses critical information. In its place there are false information, spurious issues and loaded statements supplied by the government which keep the wheels of misinformation and propaganda turning. Issues are raised which have no connection with reality or do not have as much of a connection or impact as they are made out to have.

Big political parties use fake news to destroy smaller ones. The latter, with their modest resources, are helpless, caught in the web of lies. The IT cells of powerful parties and their supporters are all engaged in disseminating false information. You could call it the equivalent of carpet bombing. Now, some political parties are constituting teams which catch fake news spread by other parties. For instance, during the elections in France, the National Front put together a Fake News Alert team. Parties in India will soon have to put together their own teams.

The volume and spate of fake news increases during election time. In 2016, when a referendum was conducted in Italy on measures that would have changed its constitution and given the prime minister greater powers, half the stories shared on Facebook were spurious and clearly designed to influence the plebiscite. Alarmed by the torrent of false stories coming from Russia—notorious for its fake news factories believed to be funded by the government—the European Union recently constituted a task force, the East StratCom Team, to counter them. This team was provided with a lot of money and resources during elections in the Netherlands and France so that they could thwart Russian propaganda. Russia has been accused of spending a lot of money on fake news in order to manipulate elections in several countries, including America.

In India, too, the quantity of fake news increases during elections. The Election Commission has no means to stem this flood. It doesn't even have a firm definition of the phenomenon. What the Commission does acknowledge is paid news, though there isn't yet a clear law to deal with that, either. The Commission creates Media Certification and Monitoring Committees at the state and district levels during every election to identify and catch paid news and issues notices to candidates asking for clarifications. In one of its reports, released in 2013, the Commission said that 1,400 instances of paid news were observed in the legislative assembly elections held in seventeen states between 2010 and 2013. The general election of 2014 threw up 787 cases of paid news. Over 3,100 paid-news related notices were issued to candidates in the 2014 elections.

The Election Commission could not stop paid news but it did manage to create an agency which goes to work after each election is notified. However, nowadays all the games have usually begun even before the election dates are announced. There isn't much for the Commission to do.

The Election Commission defines paid news as 'any news or analysis appearing in any media (print & electronic) for a price in cash or kind as consideration', and says that it 'plays a very vitiating role in the context of free and fair elections...advertisements [are published] in the garb of news items, totally misleading the electors'. But the beast has evolved and grown way beyond this. It isn't just about advertisements masquerading as news any longer. It is now the era of fake news, and no fig leaf is needed; lies are the new truth. Fake news happens on such a large scale that the government, if it really values democratic principles, must constitute a separate commission for it during elections which, like the Election Commission—a regulatory authority—should have constitutional rights and also be independent. But given the track record not just of the present government but of every government in the short history of our republic, we can be sure this won't happen in a hurry, if it happens at all.

Fake news changes the character of society; perhaps not permanently but certainly for a significant length of time. You will remember the case of the Monkey Man in Delhi back in 2001. The Monkey Man was reported, variously, as a four-foot-tall hairy creature with a steel claw, an eight-foot giant with a snout and red glowing eyes, an alien with a steel helmet and three blinking buttons on its chest. Sometimes, whatever it was, became invisible, or became a cat. Grown men and women, teenagers and children lost themselves in the imaginings of a Monkey Man. They would stay up all night, cowering in fear or armed and ready to attack and kill the monster. A panic-stricken woman woken up by her neighbours' shouting fell down the stairs and died; a man lost his life when he jumped off his balcony. A vagrant and a van-driver, both short-statured men, were chased and beaten up by mobs.

This is exactly what fake news is doing to us today. It controls our behaviour in such a way that we become robots, we cease to be citizens, individuals capable of common sense and reason. Fake news keeps us awake at night; we see communities turn on each other because of it; we see people being beaten up, even killed because of it. We let it all happen.

When a society goes collectively mad, the fallout affects the functioning of its law and order machinery. All agencies begin to react as dictated by the fake news. The Delhi Police tried to explain, quite vociferously, that no Monkey Man existed but it finally admitted defeat and announced a reward of 50,000 rupees for his capture. The home ministry was asked for help in the form of the Rapid Action Force. In view of the seriousness of the situation, a special team was put together and tasked with investigating the matter. The entire system began pursuing an untruth. Some saw the busy hand of Pakistan in the matter while others claimed it was the work of a local gang.

Pakistan returned as the Monkey Man in the Gujarat elections of 2017.

But let us return to Delhi, 2001 for now. In June that year, the Delhi Police finally solved the mystery. The report by its special committee, which included members of the Institute of Human Behaviour and the Central Forensic Laboratory, said that no Monkey Man existed at all. The then joint commissioner of police, Suresh Rai, said that no monkey, or any other animal for that matter, was the culprit. The police further said that Pakistan had no hand in the Monkey Man terror either, and no gang of hoodlums was involved. The police admitted that reckless media coverage had spread this madness. At that time, news channels had formed teams of five reporters each who would roam the streets of the city after dark looking for the Monkey Man, to get some soundbites from him. People saw these intrepid reporters out on the hunt night after night. Many among them are anchors on prime-time television today. Clearly, the practice they gained in embroidering and spreading the Monkey Man story is proving useful now.

We hadn't matured enough at the time when Monkey Man was making the rounds; which is why so many of us spent entire nights running around in confusion and jumping about to no purpose. We've made much progress since those days. We've become well-seasoned in this age of fake news. We are never in doubt. We swallow whatever we are given without question and start living with our consuming impressions and firm ideas. Our ability to digest fake news has improved and developed greatly.

Which is why, in November 2016, long queues formed up in front of shops in many Indian states for sugar and salt. A message had arrived on WhatsApp announcing that there would soon be a severe shortage of sugar and salt. People of Delhi, Lucknow, Kolkata and Hyderabad turned in a good performance in the case, along with people from the smaller towns. The then chief minister of Uttar Pradesh, Akhilesh Yadav, kept saying that this was a rumour and instructed government officials to take strict action against rumour-mongers. How nice it is that there is punishment for rumour-mongers but none for those who believe in them. The chief minister of Delhi, Arvind Kejriwal, and the Union minister for consumer affairs, food and public distribution, Ram Vilas Paswan, issued statements that there was no shortage of salt. But the rumours, as is their wont these days, WhatsApped their way—encrypted end-to-end—to Mumbai, and salt soared to 200 rupees a kilogramme. The Mumbai Police was also forced to tweet that this was a rumour. Nothing worked. News arrived from many places that shopkeepers were selling salt at prices as high as 600 rupees a kilo. There were reports that a woman had died in a stampede outside a shop in Kanpur.

Fake news can also be used to falsify history. Powerful sections of the polity launch many false versions of history. Entire organizations are enlisted for this exercise, which makes it impossible for any single historian to challenge and refute the information that is put out there. Since May 2014, textbooks have been rewritten in many states. But the real mischief with history happens on social media, which is awash with false histories. It is the malice in these campaigns that needs to be examined.

The prime target of most purveyors of fake history who are champions of our present regime is Jawaharlal Nehru, the first prime minister of India. On 15 May 2016, Amulya Gopalakrishnan of the *Times of India* published a report on the kinds of lies being spread about Nehru:

- Jawahar is a word borrowed from the Arabic; no Kashmiri Brahmin will give his son an Arabic name.
- Nehru's grandfather was called Ghiyasuddin Ghazi; he was a police officer during the Mughal era and he renamed himself Gangadhar Nehru.
- Nehru was born in a red-light area in Allahabad.
- Nehru impregnated a Catholic nun. The church sent the nun out of India for which Nehru remained grateful to the church all his life.

Such hate-fuelled misinformation about Nehru was presented in the garb of news so that lakhs of people would consume it and hatred for him would spread widely. A video was put out in which it was said that he died of AIDS. He was shown as a debauched philanderer with the aid of doctored pictures with Jacqueline Kennedy and Mrinalini Sarabhai. Photoshop was freely used. Information on Wikipedia about Jawaharlal Nehru and his father Motilal Nehru was edited and changed. *The Times of India*, quoting Pranesh Prakash of the Centre for Internet and Society, reported that these edits on Wikipedia originated from a government of India IP address.

In January 2016, the Narendra Modi government released previously classified documents related to Netaji Subhas Chandra Bose. Nothing of significance was revealed but simultaneously, a letter said to be written by Nehru in 1945 to the British prime minister Attlee was circulated on WhatsApp. In the letter, Nehru refers to Bose as a 'war criminal'. The letter was fake—unsigned and full of spelling and factual errors—but many journalists were fooled. Leading newspapers and magazines of the country and several websites carried the letter—different versions, with different dates and different errors. When they discovered it was fabricated—which should have been apparent to any serious journalist even at a glance—everyone started to delete the letter and apologize.

The internet is being filled with fake information about Nehru. When your child downloads this information for her school or college project or exam, she will write the wrong answers. It is possible that her teachers, inspired by a particular political ideology, will mark her well on those incorrect answers. And she will grow up believing that what she knows is the truth, when it is not. She may be an ideal citizen as long as the present BJP government rules. But regimes change, countries change. How would she have been equipped to deal with a future where some other kinds of lies become the official narrative? And how will she handle any kind of truth? Will she always live in a bubble, cut off from reality?

It was with the aid of fake news that the most heinous violence in the history of mankind was sought to be erased. Hitler had millions of Jews murdered in gas chambers, an event we know as the Holocaust. A programme to make this truth vanish from the internet was put in motion. It was fortunate that Carole Cadwalladr of *The Guardian* noticed it. When Carole typed 'Did the Holocaust Really Happen?' into the Google taskbar, the reply that it threw up was that it didn't. The search engine also took her to the neo-Nazi website www.stormfront.org on which were listed ten reasons why the Holocaust could never have happened.

On 11 December 2016 Carole wrote a long piece for *The Guardian*. She reported that there are many such denial videos on YouTube too. This when it is a recorded fact, in books as well as historical documents, that Hitler had 6 million people killed. Till at least 2013, some survivors of Nazi concentration camps were still alive. After Carole raised these questions, Google did make amendments, but think of how many historical facts must have been similarly changed, how much history is likely being erased even as you read this. Just as it is being transformed with the aid of TV channels which play before our eyes every day.

Here's another interesting fact: Tom Reilly of *The Sun Chronicle* wrote in an editorial on 29 June 2017 that even a massive news organization like the Associated Press has fallen victim to fake news. This is an organization that is 171 years old, and has 243 news bureaus in 120 countries. Over 1,700 newspapers and 5,000 TV and radio networks around the world source news from it. Associated Press has accepted that some of the news it put out in recent times was fake. It has now started a news feature called 'Not Real News'. This feature will reveal the truth about those nuggets of false news which go viral on Twitter and other platforms. But this is like cleaning a large lake with a small strainer.

Rumours and fake news have always been the preferred weapons of fascists and majoritarian fundamentalists in democracies. By inciting mobs to fulfil their agendas, they use democracy to subvert and destroy democracy itself. Their perverse logic is this: if democracy is the will of the majority, is not a mob the majority? And which political party can afford to criticize democracy? They also know that a mob cannot be named, arrested, tried and convicted, so murder and intimidation can carry on unchecked.

The web of lies, the motivated twisting of facts, the building of false narratives—none of this happens overnight. It is done over months and years and on a large scale. It begins at the top, in the corridors of power. The results are seen in the streets. After months of malicious propaganda about cow slaughter, a man was pulled out of his house and lynched by a mob of several hundred people, many of whom had been his neighbours for years.

Two days after Mohammad Akhlaq was killed, on the night of 28 September 2015, I was in his village, Bisada, in Dadri, Uttar Pradesh. I remember the door of his room.

The mob had broken down the door with such animal force that instead of giving way at its hinges, it had split right down the middle. They had bashed his head with a sewing machine before dragging him out with his son for the public lynching. Akhlaq was beaten to pulp, he was dead in a few minutes. Bricks were smashed on his son's head; he regained consciousness after several weeks in hospital and multiple surgeries. Akhlaq's eighty-two-year-old mother was beaten too. When I met her, she had deep wounds around her eyes.

Could such fury, such bestial savagery have ridden on just a rumour that Akhlaq had eaten beef? Bisada village had no history of communal tensions that could explain the killing. Akhlaq's was the only Muslim family in the village, they had lived there for over sixty years. The family home sat right in the middle of a Rajput settlement. Surely this meant there must have been a semblance of harmony there. Then how could a single, mysterious announcement from the village temple about the killing of a calf lead to such horrific mob violence within fifteen or twenty minutes?

Since then there have been regular lynchings and public beatings of Muslims and Dalits. Everywhere, it is the same story that can at any moment set fire to our country. An announcement is made on a loudspeaker. WhatsApp is used to spread doctored videos of cow slaughter. A calf goes missing. People get angry. Then pieces of meat are discovered, sometimes outside a temple, sometimes outside a Muslim home. Politicians spew venom, and a thoroughly communalized media broadcasts conspiracy theories...

Fake news can be used to trigger a mob not only against helpless minorities but also prominent ideological opponents. By the time that person disputes the news, the mob will have burned down his or her house on the basis of malicious rumours. The writer Arundhati Roy has long been a critic of right-wing politics and of army presence in Kashmir. On 17 May 2017, the actor and BJP member of Parliament Paresh Rawal tweeted that Arundhati Roy had said in an interview given in Srinagar to a Pakistani journalist that 'the 70-lakh strong Indian Army cannot defeat the azadi gang of Kashmir'. And in a subsequent tweet he wrote, 'Instead of tying stone pelter on the army jeep tie Arundhati Roy.' He was referring to the incident of an unarmed Kashmiri civilian being tied to the front of a jeep by some Indian Army jawans as a human shield against stone-pelting protestors.

This was an extremely dangerous action, especially for a sitting member of Parliament. It was an incitement to assault Arundhati Roy, or anyone else for that matter, who did not agree with the government and bigoted hyper nationalists. Many big-banner news channels actually held debates over the matter. This, when Arundhati Roy had neither visited Srinagar in the recent past nor spoken about Kashmir to any newspaper. She had indeed given an interview to *Outlook* magazine a year earlier, but Paresh Rawal's tweet was not about that, and she hadn't, even then, used the exact words attributed to her. When thewire.in discovered how the false information reached Paresh Rawal, one more deadly aspect of fake news came to the fore.

Paresh Rawal's tweet about Arundhati Roy's supposed interview linked to a post on the Facebook page called The Indian Nationalist. The 'news' had reached that page from a website called postcard.news—many of the articles on this site have been controversial for having been proved fake. According to a 17 May story by 'Aishwarya S' on postcard.news, Arundhati Roy had given the interview to 'the Pakistan newspaper *The Times of Islamabad*'. The story carried no link to the interview, but as thewire.in investigated further, it found that 'the *identical story* was published on the same day under the byline "Anand" on another Hindutva-oriented fake news site, satyavijayi.com, and under the byline "Ankita K" in a third Hindutva fake news site, theindianvoice.com. Other fake news sites that ran the identical story were theresurgentindia.com, revoltpress.com, virathindurashtra.com, while a fifth fake news site, internethindu.in, ran a slightly different version but, helpfully, provided a link to the Times of Islamabad source'.

The Times of Islamabad turned out to be a website, not a newspaper. It merely credited its 'News Desk' with the story, but thewire.in found that a similar story aired on Pakistan's Geo TV gave the source as Kashmir Media Service, which is not a media organization but 'the propaganda arm of a Kashmiri militant organization in Pakistan-occupied Kashmir. It maintains a website but the news about an Arundhati Roy interview is not archived there'. Clearly, there had never been any such interview.

So a fake interview and a nugget of fake news originating on a Pakistani fake news website ended up on the Twitter handle of an Indian Member of Parliament and a fierce debate against Arundhati Roy raged on Indian television channels, some of whom, ironically, make a virtue of Pakistan bashing.

Paresh Rawal, very reluctantly, deleted his tweet some days later. But the websites which carried the fake news did not immediately remove it. Think about how dangerous this is. Websites in Pakistan and India can actually collaborate with each other in the generation of fake news. Someone publishes a fake interview in your name on a Pakistani website; by the time you make an explanation, TV channels, political leaders and these very same websites will have ganged up together and done you tremendous harm, brought a violent mob to your door. Until now, this process has been used to scare people who raise their voices in dissent, to terrify a weak and cowardly political opposition, but soon, this strategy will be used to fix us all. Actually, it is being done already. The evidence is all around us.

Such politically motivated fake news not only removes the citizenry from its reality, it also creates a wide schism between the citizenry and those who ask questions on its behalf. It constantly perpetuates a system of intimidation, harassment and humiliation so that the collective of people who ask questions keeps shrinking and scattering. Political leaders and fundamentalist ideologues are cleverly programming us. Unless we learn to test every image, every so-called truth that we are fed, fake news will be of great use for a very long time to all those who want to keep the participants of this democracy insecure. Citizen or robot; democracy or tyranny—the choice is ours.

The National Project for Instilling Fear

In 2017, in just a span of a few months, we journalists were forced to gather twice to condemn violence against colleagues. I base this essay on two speeches I gave, in outrage and in grief; one after Basit Malik was beaten up by a mob in New Delhi, and the other after Gauri Lankesh was murdered in Bengaluru.

In June 2017, the speaker of the Lok Sabha, Sumitra Mahajan, advised us journalists to 'be like Narada' at an event in New Delhi. Do not report unpleasant truths, she said. If you must speak to the government, do so in beautiful language.

In Indian mythology, the sage Narada, with his chant of 'Narayan Narayan', is a traveller who bears news to different realms and is among the most ardent devotees of Lord Vishnu. 'If you want to see us journalists as Narada,' I wanted to tell Madam Speaker at that time, 'you must give us at least a glimpse of the divine faces in the king's court. Who among them are worthy of being gods, for whom we would be willing to become Narada and refrain from voicing unpleasant truths?' And I also wanted to ask her, 'How is it that *you* get to decide what is or is not a pleasant truth?'

The project to browbeat journalists into submission has only gained momentum over the last few years. Journalists are finding it difficult to track who is being targeted and for what. From the lanes to the crossroads, there is a mob lying in wait; it recognizes us by face. And at the least sign that anyone is doing her or his job as a journalist, the mob first looks at that person with suspicion and it then attacks.

On 9 June 2017, Basit Malik, a reporter for *Caravan* magazine, was set upon by a mob—after his name identified him as Muslim—while on assignment at Sonia Vihar in Delhi and handed over to the police, who were told that he was a 'Pakistani' and had been caught 'without papers'. He has written about his ordeal in the *Caravan.* There is one man in Basit's terrifying account who stands out above everyone else, a lawyer. This presence is an unmistakable one in most incidents of mob violence nowadays. In a way, he can be described as a 'legal empowerment cell' for the mob. Several such incidents involving lawyers in recent times come to mind.

For instance, in February 2016, two journalists from

the *Indian Express*, Alok Singh and Kaunain Sheriff, were covering the sedition case against Kanhaiya Kumar, former president of the Jawaharlal Nehru University Students' Union, when they were accused of being 'anti-national' and attacked by lawyers inside the Patiala House court complex in Delhi. We will perhaps never know what really transpired there. Then, in Kochi, July 2016, journalists at the Kerala High Court were prevented from covering a case involving a government pleader by a violent mob of lawyers.

What K.B. Koliwad, the speaker of the Karnataka Assembly, did in June 2017—sentencing the editors of *Yelahanka Voice* and *Hi Bangalore*, to a prison term of one year and imposing a fine of Rs 10,000 each for 'publishing defamatory articles against legislators'—was also just one more example among many of browbeating.

And consider what Asad Ashraf, Anupam Pandey and Vinay Pandey, journalists who were arrested in Hanumangarh while investigating arms training camps allegedly being conducted by the Bajrang Dal, had to endure in Rajasthan. The policeman who said, 'I will be suspended from the force today but I will still beat you with my shoes,' was emboldened only because he knew that the authority which manages the National Project for Instilling Fear is his political lord and master and has his back.

The National Project for Instilling Fear has reached completion in India. Before new highways and jobs, everybody has been unfailingly given one thing—fear. For every individual—whether a journalist or anyone else—fear is now a daily reality and we are all experiencing it in many different ways. From the moment we step out of our homes, warnings ring in our ears: be careful, look here, look there.

It is obvious that the 'godi' media is the only one which is safe in India today. If you jump into the lap of authority and snuggle down in it, nobody anywhere will dare say anything to you. All you need to do is to lose yourself in songs of devotion, strum the tanpura like Narada did, and chant 'Narayan Narayan' on the television screen.

Let me tell you about an incident about a friend who was travelling by train with his mother. A woman of conservative views, she was wearing a burqa. A mob formed instantaneously and spewed taunts at them throughout the duration of the journey. Their self-confidence was shattered within the first couple of hours. In this project for instilling fear, which is now being successfully implemented on a national scale, individuals comprise the smallest and the most vulnerable units. And now the project has reached the newsroom and individuals within it too. I have no idea how this situation will improve. Maybe we can create a helpline for those who have been beaten up and for the families of those who have died.

Certain sections of the mainstream media have always been in the firing line of hatemongers, it is now also the turn of many of our comrades practising alternative journalism to become targets—those who are running small websites with a handful of journalists. These are websites that receive maybe a lakh or two or five lakh hits. When all mainstream voices are muzzled, it is these websites which report incidents. These journalists too are going to be beaten senseless. All this is happening systematically as part of the political game plan.

Many local political agents who play the role of vendors, 'feeding' information through WhatsApp, are now in the business of killing as well. Once, gathering ten men to beat someone to death used to take time. In Basit Malik's case, it would have taken no time to assemble a crowd because they have the perfect apparatus: WhatsApp—which rules out field reporting for most.

I speak from experience; in the days following demonetization, it became very difficult to go anywhere to report from the field. You are not going to travel with a squad of Special Protection Group personnel, right?

Under these circumstances, where is one to go and, in the minimum time, accomplish the task of speaking to as many people as possible? It is up to us to find a way of dealing with this fear.

It has become necessary to tell people, 'What you are watching on television is garbage! You are not being readied to kill Muslims. One day you will be used to kill just about anybody.' Convert every person in a mob into a possible killer—this too is an ongoing project.

We are not just fighting against the muzzling of debate so essential to a democracy. Our problem is that very soon we will not be able to step out even in our own neighbourhood. You may think a person who is a well-known face is at greater risk. Was Basit Malik a well-known face? We have reached a stage where at the mere sight of the Urdu script written somewhere, we will start trashing it on the grounds that it is a 'Pakistani' language.

The fact that many journalists did not attend the solidarity meeting for Basit Malik gave those of us who had gathered a great deal of concern. Their lack of response made us feel that there is a pact of silence about incidents such as these. I often find myself in the midst of many such journalists and I detect no unease, no restlessness in them. It is a warning sign when an assault on a colleague leaves you unmoved, for it means that even the basic spirit of solidarity is lost to us.

At that time, when Basit Malik was attacked, it felt as if what we needed was a weekly calendar of meetings to protest assaults on journalists, so regular they had become. And a chilling fear set in that we would soon be seeing each other at condolence meetings.

Then, on 5 September 2017, Gauri Lankesh, journalist, activist and editor of the Kannada weekly *Lankesh Patrike*, was shot down by bike-borne assailants in front of her house in Bengaluru. The motive for that murder wasn't clear then, and perhaps we will never know it. From the time that that news arrived, I began to notice how many murderers there are among us. On the timelines on social media and on Twitter emerged a horde of murderers—and those who support that mindset which endorses murder. Who, without shame, hesitation, or a sense of boundaries, attached various questions as riders to her murder and termed it legitimate. That horde brought up the question of Pandits in Kashmir, the question of the killings of RSS workers in Kerala—that horde demanded answers to each question before the answer to the murder could be sought.

And while efforts were being made to distract from the issue at hand, what was important for us to do was to stay united and concentrate on the question of Gauri Lankesh's murder and make demands of the authorities. Would the crime be investigated? Would Siddaramaiah, the chief minister of Karnataka, do that? But he had done nothing about the killing of M.M. Kalburgi—the noted scholar and academic, former vice-chancellor of Kannada University, and a strident voice against superstition in Hinduism. Had Siddaramaiah wanted, he could have fought openly, on the frontlines, and ensured that the Kalburgi case was professionally investigated and reached it to its logical conclusion. He didn't. Which also didn't mean that those in power in neighbouring Maharashtra had done any better in the matters of the murders of Narendra Dabholkar and Govind Pansare, the well-known rationalists and advocates of reform in the Hindu religion. It is depressingly clear that the government—parcelled out among whichever parties—is ranged against us all.

I don't think it has ever happened anywhere that so many people have publicly justified a murder as vociferously and boldly, and with as much poison, as Gauri's was. And I was saddened most of all by the fact that the man who had been lovingly given the seat of power by the people of India, that man was a Twitter follower of Nikhil Dadhich, who described Gauri Lankesh, a recently deceased woman, as a 'bitch'. Dadhich said in a Tweet, 'Now that a bitch has died a dog's death, all the puppies are mewling in one voice.' I was disappointed in our Prime Minister.

Our Prime Minister can have any number of complaints about this country, but he cannot complain that Indian citizens have held anything back in how they have granted him power. The citizenry has given him the sort of majority that he demanded of them, even more, in every state and in every place. I wanted our Prime Minister to tell us how he came to that point: when he can barely afford to sleep a few hours in his quest to serve the nation—as his propaganda team tells us—how does he find the time to follow people like Dadhich on Twitter? I also hoped that whenever he returned from his travels at that time, he should unfollow Dadhich. He never did.

We should all, as citizens of this country, ask the following questions of our Prime Minister: 'Why do you follow Dadhich? What does he contribute that the thirty percent of the population which voted for you cannot? Is it this man, or someone like him, who makes you victorious? Is such a man necessary for you to reach that position of power? And now that Dadhich and others like him are in the Club of 1700 whom you follow on Twitter, can you not ask them, "Did you boys have no sense of my dignity, the prime minister of the nation?" '

If he cannot find anyone else in India to follow on Twitter, I offer the Prime Minister my handle; he can follow me. I assure him that I will criticize him with great respect. He will never feel that I have insulted him. I will quote beautiful poems to him, and many shlokas from the Hindu scriptures. He will not feel at all that he lives in an India where he is not held in esteem.

Someone at the condolence meeting for Gauri Lankesh asked me, 'What are you here for?'

We hadn't gathered there for ourselves. We were there because the message that was being sent out to everyone by killing Gauri Lankesh was that we should all keep quiet or we would meet the same fate as her. We gathered to condemn a society which will look upon a corpse laid out before it and laugh. We gathered to assert that this is not our way, it is not the way of the India we know. We gathered to resolve that we send this message clearly, to whichever government is in power up there. And to tell ourselves that this is something they must listen to, and understand. We gathered to find ways so that we do not have to come together time and again to offer condolences and tributes. We had gathered to share our deep concerns and fears. We had also gathered to examine the many ways we were drifting away and see the harm that would come with disunity. We were there to understand that to cast a veil upon the doings of the government, from a sense of political and ideological loyalties, is not a good thing. We were there also to hold guilty those who protest only for the sake of protesting and those who support only for the sake of supporting. We were there to remind ourselves that despite the best efforts of that National Project for Instilling Fear, we should not give in.

For a few days after Gauri was murdered, I walked around terrified. It felt as if someone had riddled me with bullets and people were shuffling past my corpse. Numerous well-wishers, readers and viewers from all over the country called me, telling me to stop being a lone voice. 'You will meet the same fate. Write to the home minister, the prime minister, ask for security.' I wanted to tell them, arre bhai, when they haven't been able to provide security even to their own toadies, how will I receive any?

A particular kind of political atmosphere has been created, through the National Project for Instilling Fear, which offers divisive forces all kinds of support. All of those who were laughing at the killing of Gauri Lankesh are a product of that atmosphere. This is a shameful development. Which face, which facet of Hindutva is this? That a brave, idealistic and peaceful person is killed and we laugh, and say that she was a bitch who deserved to die? This is that same section of society which said nothing in support of the two women who spoke up against Gurmeet Ram Rahim. Can we name any secretary of any Women's Commission who supported those two women? Do we know of any minister, soldier, general secretary, secretary who tweeted about those two women? It was thanks to the battles waged by them that the empire of such a powerful baba was destroyed. But our society, and the responsible people within it, support the sentiment of 'beti bachao, beti padhao'—save daughters, educate daughters—only at the level of a slogan.

We must also never forget that the journalist who was murdered was a woman. In this country, it is with great difficulty that a few women reach that position from where they, with the keenness of their views, can show a mirror to society and to the government. For Gauri to reach that point after a long battle, and for her to be cut down at that point was naturally an immense waste of a talent.

When even those who follow and support the Prime Minister—and who are in turn endorsed by him—do not heed his dignity, know that a mob of lunatics, armed with manufactured opinions and primed by fake news, has risen amongst us. That mob will surround us and kill us—whether we are alone, or we number in the thousands.

The question is not one of personal survival—that is there, obviously—but of the citizens out there, who fight a daily battle to get themselves heard on prime time, who want their questions to be raised, their ideals reinforced. Whose voices are being drowned in the din of fake news and spurious issues, whose questions are being ignored and whose restlessness is being quelled. People's desires and aspirations are being constantly murdered. Fake news, incidentally, was what Gauri Lankesh's final editorial spoke of. About how fake news is not only a Delhi-centric phenomenon, but is creating havoc in the states too, where it is steadily dividing people into the binary of Hindu and Muslim.

We must understand the deadly patterns of fear and violence and hate that are being woven around all of us; for they are what Gauri Lankesh fell prey to, a brave journalist.

Wherever a Mob Gathers Is Hitler's Germany

I wrote this essay soon after 4 July 2017, the day Prime Minister Modi visited the Yad Vashem Holocaust Memorial on his official tour of Israel. We should be grateful that he did. With his visit, the Prime Minister not only offered tributes to the Jews who were massacred during that fateful time, he also dismissed the legacy of that murderer, Hitler.

When the heads of state visit other countries, the visit is not only for their own sakes, citizens also have a chance to learn much. I myself was particularly grateful because, after his visit, I found the opportunity to read extensively about this important chapter in modern history, especially one specific episode within it, and understand its significance as a cautionary tale, both for contemporary India and the world. To read and understand this chapter is important particularly for the young, I think, for these events happened much before they were born and they must—we all must—realize that those of us who do not learn lessons from history will become assassins for the history that is yet to be recorded.

———

Of all the nights in Germany, the one between 9 and 10 November 1938 was one of the ghastliest—the 'Crystal Night' or the 'Night of Broken Glass'. That was the night when the fully planned campaign to persecute Jews was put into motion on the ground; to massacre them, to take away everything that they owned, to force them out from the country.

In the years leading up to 1938, concerted programmes had been set up to drive Jewish businessmen and traders out of Germany. Jewish doctors and lawyers were financially boycotted. Jews were ordered to write the letter 'J' on their passports. Men were ordered to add 'Israel' to their names and women 'Sarah' so that they could be easily identified as being Jewish. The professors of the universities of Germany also played an active role in the spreading of hatred. In their classrooms they taught character and psychological analyses of Jews which painted them in an evil light. The bureaucracy kept busy issuing Bills which would identify Jews, or wipe out their fundamental rights. Police would arrest anyone who spoke in favour of the Jews. Jews were forbidden from entering public parks in the city. People stopped patronizing stores owned by Jews. Shopfronts were marked to identify their owners as Jews. Coaches in trains were segregated. Germany had always been an integrated community in which Jews lived along with everyone else. Plans were made to pluck them out and send them into ghettoes outside the city, ghettoes which, in a cruel irony, wealthy Jews would eventually be made to pay for. Insurance companies were ordered not to compensate Jews for damage to their houses, shops and stores. Efforts were made to isolate Jews in every which way so that the mob which was out to get them would find it easy.

These were the many grave but scattered and diverse incidents of violence which had been taking place in the years leading up to 1938. Some people supported these incidents, others opposed them, and, in the acts of support and protest, the populace was being numbed to violence, and being prepared mentally to become the murderers of the future and fulfil the propaganda that was being fed them. By then, many Germans had started taking pride in becoming a part of different armies and organizations and shouting 'Heil Hitler!' They had become bhakts of Hitler, and he had injected the poison of violence in their minds. Hitler's own obsession had become the people's obsession. And Hitler himself had to do nothing; the German people would do everything. All that Hitler and his government needed to do was to allow people to act as they pleased.

'We should be very clear that, in the next decade, we

are going to face an extremely sensitive clash. One which has not been ever heard about. This is not a clash only of nations but also a struggle with the ideologies of the Jews, Freemasons, Marxists and the churches. I believe that the soul of these powers resides in the Jews, who are the root of all negativity. The Jews believe that if Germany and Italy are not destroyed, they will themselves be annihilated. This is a question that has remained before us for many years. We will force the Jews out of Germany. We will inflict such cruelty upon them as has never ever been imagined by anyone.' Heinrich Himmler, one of the leaders of the SS, proclaimed this in a speech to other leaders of the organization a few days before the events of 9–10 November 1938 so that they too could be primed for violence against the Jews.

Hitler's whip-smart and murderous propaganda manager, Joseph Goebbels was to relay the news about the violence back to Hitler. Hitler's silence, and the occasional verbal order to intensify the campaign were to serve as directions to the governmental machinery that the massacre should be allowed to continue. The executors of this campaign were the mob and the SS—Schutzstaffel—an army whose youthful members had been shown, along with everyone else, dreams of a Grand Germany, a Superpower Germany, Germany, the Emperor of Europe.

On the night of 7 November 1938, the third legation secretary of Germany, Ernst vom Rath was murdered in Paris. The assassin was Herschel Grynszpan, a Jew of Polish origin. For Goebbels it was as if the gods in the heavens had accepted his prayers. The fuse had long been smoldering, all that was needed was a wind to fan it to life and they had found it.

Goebbels wrote in his diary that night: 'I attend a party programme in the old town hall. There is a large crowd. I explain all of Hitler's thoughts to them. He decides that demonstrations against the Jews should carry on, says that police should be ordered to back down; let the Jews face the people's rage. I urgently issue orders to the police and the party. I then speak for a little while at the party programme. There is much applause. I then immediately pick up the phone. Now the people will go to work.'

The mob was let loose. Not only was the police ordered to step aside—while being made the nodal agency of the massacre—in cases where Jewish-owned stores were to be burned down, they were to take owners into 'protective custody' so that the arson could be carried out properly. The fire services were ordered to ignore the burning houses belonging to Jews and to douse the houses next door to them with water so that property belonging to people of Aryan origins could be preserved.

Everything was arranged in such a manner that it would seem as if this was a natural, spontaneous anger on the part of the people. So that no blame could be laid at the government's or at the police force's doorsteps. The game which was played in the name of the 'people's anger' smeared blood on the face of history which yet hasn't washed off. And this happened in an age when modernism was in its vibrant youth in Europe and the idea of democracy was being feted and paraded.

Hundreds of Jews were murdered that night. Women and children were grievously injured. Nearly a hundred places of worship were destroyed. On the night of 9 November the Munich synagogue was burnt down by the Nazi army. The excuse given was that the synagogue was obstructing traffic. Fifteen synagogues were burnt down in Berlin alone. Cemeteries were attacked. Thousands of shops and stores were burned down. Countless apartments were reduced to rubble. The pavements of large cities in Germany were strewn with shattered glass. So were the streets in front of shops. Every thing, every object associated with the memory of Jews was destroyed, even their private photographs. Many men and women committed suicide. Many were injured who later died. The police forcibly pushed 30,000 Jew men out of the country and into concentration camps. Since there wasn't enough space, only men and wealthy Jews were picked up. That night, when Goebbels returned to his hotel room, the sound of shattering windows could be heard. He wrote in his diary: 'Excellent work! Excellent work!' He also wrote: 'The German people will forever remember what it means to assassinate a German diplomat.'

That which had not been ordered by the authorities was also carried out and nothing was said about that which was carried out. There was a silence which lay over the land like a suffocating blanket. This was done by managing the press. There was a binding agreement that wherever Hitler went, the press would not ask him questions about the violence that had been unleashed against the Jews. Hitler was to remain silent so that his image in the world would not be tarnished.

Hitler had become enamoured by the German mob. For the mob had been tailored to his needs. And, inspired by the mob, Hitler passed a unique new law—Jews would have to themselves pay for the damage caused to them. As if they had themselves set their shops and houses on fire. When the mob creates its own empire, evil principles begin to rule hearts and minds.

The success of the Nazi regime in its murderous campaign was largely because of propaganda. Only one singular narrative was stated and promoted in every which way. Any other narrative was allowed no existence at all. People were steadily moulded by the propaganda and they did not realize that they had been transformed into a weapon. Propaganda has only one purpose—the construction of a mob. It is the mob which carries out the killings and blood splatters the clothes of only those who make up the mob. The government and the leaders all appear blameless. No one questions the role of propaganda in bringing mobs together. And no one investigates the kind of poison that fills the minds of the people in those mobs.

'The radicalization encountered no opposition of any weight.' I found this profound and chilling sentence in one of the books I read to understand the story of the Crystal Night. Chilling because I realized that it was yet another way in which history keeps repeating itself. No one protested against Hitler's mob army in any way. The common people kept expressing their shame and regret about all that had happened but also kept describing themselves as having been helpless. Those who could speak, kept quiet. The church, which teaches 'Thou shalt love thy neighbour', was quiet too. Many countries of the world refused to give shelter to fleeing Jews. Isn't that what happens everywhere even today?

It is thus my fervent prayer that we stop to think about the nature of violence. We must understand that the world is still culpable for what happened to the Jews, whatever image Israel presently has: as a country which Palestine accuses of cruelty and of being a perpetrator of massacres. And perhaps, as we think carefully, we will find out why it is that a society which has endured severe violence seeks to inflict as severe or even worse violence upon others. And we will also see, more clearly than ever, why Mahatma Gandhi laid such stress upon ahimsa. Non-violence is the only way out of the black cycle of hatred. It is the only way in which we can look out into the world and find it coloured in the singular hue of love.

We must also strive to understand the nature of mobs. A mob has its own constitution. It has its own country. It drafts its own orders and directives, and identifies its own prey. And knowing the nature of mobs, we must resolve to allow institutions to complete their duties of investigation and accountability. We must accept, with patience and conviction, that they who are accused will be investigated and punished. To become a mob, at any place, at any time, is to become Hitler's Germany.

Being the People

In 2014, a new national curriculum was launched, and the lapdog media has been working overtime to help implement it. Although the overall theme remains the same, the chapters vary. Every evening is devoted to one or the other: khichdi-biryani, Taj Mahal-mandir, Nehru versus Patel, Bose versus Nehru, triple talaq, Akbar, Aurangzeb, Shah Jahan, Ashok, Tipu Sultan, Rani Padmavati, the tallest statue in the world, and a variety of great men who are brought into and taken out of the curriculum when the imagination fails.

It feels as if the entire nation is sitting in a history class and all of us are studying history for the very first time. The troll, the 'bhakt' and the news anchor are our historians—the news anchor above all. The national-level 'lectures' of the news anchors have one basic idea—all of them have latched on to the notion that some 'great man' or the other has been ignored, wiped out of history, and we must ensure that he—almost always a 'he'—gets the recognition he has been denied. His aspirations will finally be fulfilled; but he is long gone, he is just a pretext for fulfilling the aspirations of those who have set the curriculum and those who disseminate it.

The moment we start wondering what is going on, pat comes a mention of Chankaya on WhatsApp. He's the showstopper, the benchmark of professorship in our new national curriculum. Anything goes in his name. Especially on issues pertaining to history, war, statecraft and politics. If you want to say something that has no basis in fact, attribute it to Chanakya. People will fall for it hook, line and sinker. Be sure to add a sprinkling of catchwords like the nation and, yes, valour—catchwords that are connected to the idea of physical bravery and sundry things that go with it. Then start sharing your nugget.

The entire political debate taking place in our midst is built around this national curriculum. We are under the impression that by means of this curriculum we are being connected to history, when in fact we are being deviously cut off from it. We are being stripped of history. The process of writing history does not proceed in a single, straight line. This process does not end at any specific point; it is always a work in progress—one book prompts ten more publications; one piece of research is challenged by newer ones. There is no one Marxist or Left history that comes straight out of the party headquarters as a clear line in bold letters. In contrast, right-wing history clearly seems to emerge from one source. If you want me to come with you to a library to prove what I have just said, I'm prepared to do so.

History-writing is marked by constant change and churn. It has stepped out of the lives of kings and queens and great men to grasp the nuances of our regular lives and our everyday achievements. It has tried to understand history in the context of how we live, how we view the times we live in. The attempt has been to make history-writing a well-rounded exercise, to the extent it is supported by documentary and other archival material.

Now once again there is a move to drag history-writing back to the chronicles of kings and queens. It is reckless myth-making, fuelled by the idea of retribution—the 'faithful', the 'true Hindus', will avenge the deeds, real and imagined, of those who are no longer in our midst. The idea of vengeance persists even though those who exist in the present have nothing to do with that history and are not responsible for any of it.

Through these narratives of the new national curriculum, young hearts are being filled with the flames of hatred; they are being transformed into human bombs walking in our midst. Communalism turns human beings into bombs—we will see this change not just in our neighbour's child but also in our own. When a youth filled with pure hatred chances upon an ordinary quarrel between two individuals who happen to be from different faiths, he can only see the incident with a communal eye and explode, human bomb that he is. He becomes a participant in the act of killing; part of the crowd that kills a Pehlu Khan or Muhammad Akhlaq or Junaid Khan, knowing he will never be punished by the powers that be. This is the kind of human bomb we have in our midst today. We are no longer a weak-hearted people; now that 1,200 years of slavery and sixty years of sickularism and bad governance are behind us, we have produced our own Jihadi John, who hacks and burns a man to death and releases the video on the internet.

As these human bombs increase in numbers in any society or nation, it is not the state that stands to lose but all of us—our status and power as citizens will correspondingly shrink. When we watch television images of a person beaten to pulp by a crowd—he may be of any religion—the moment at which the victim is overpowered by the crowd leaves us shaken and afraid even though we are watching the news in the safety of our home. We are wary of sharing our feelings on Facebook and hesitate to step out of the house at certain times. We feel intimidated and our civil rights as citizens get eroded.

Our minds are being filled with hatred not only for the sole purpose of perpetuating the hold of a particular party or ideology on power but to ensure the complete decimation of the power that comes with being the citizens of a democracy. I earnestly urge you to keep your child safe from the ill-effects of the new national curriculum on social media and prime-time television, and keep yourself out of its reach as well. The national curriculum is virulent in its theme, and unrelenting. It has a predictable pattern—wherever there is an election, it makes its presence felt. All of us need to have the self-confidence that is part of the consciousness of being the people of a strong civilization, a rich and diverse culture. Just as justice and injustice are part of our present, so it was in the past. We need to learn to deal with it. We should know how to negotiate history. But these debates are pushing us to the farthest extremes; consequently, we are moving inexorably towards communalization—an ever-widening gulf of mistrust with regard to a particular community.

In schools all over Germany, children are educated on how to deal with the blot on their past because of Hitler and his Nazi regime, one of the most evil in all history. This is a stigma that cannot be removed either by tearing out or burning those pages of history, or by running away and hiding from it. I once asked a German journalist if they were overcome by a sense of guilt.

Mentioning that politicians in my country didn't think twice about casually branding anybody as Hitler, I asked her if that were so in Germany as well. She replied, 'We are very careful about how we bring Hitler's name into any debate; only an individual who loses the ability to offer a reasoned and human argument is thought to possess a Hitlerian streak.'

She recalled that around the time the film *Schindler's List*, set in Nazi Germany, was released, their teacher spoke to them. This is what the teacher said: 'The film dwells on the darkest chapter in the history of our nation. Yes, it did happen, but we are not to blame—neither your father nor mine. We ought to be ashamed of this dark chapter of our history and we are, but when we watch the film we shall not be wracked by guilt or anger. Rather, we shall experience a sense of self-confidence that we are no longer trapped in that time; we have come a long way from that juncture and are living in a new age.'

We in India have not educated our citizens on ways to negotiate history. On the contrary, the narrative that is being created as a 'tradition', especially through our television channels, is one of inhumanity. Perhaps many will dismiss these words of caution, calling me alarmist. But there will come a time when we will recall these words in distress—if not for ourselves, then for our children, for no one among us wants to see our child pick up a sword to kill a neighbour. Our child may well be saved by the party he owes allegiance to, but we will not get a moment's sleep knowing that our child is a murderer.

When Pehlu Khan was lynched in Alwar, there was little reaction on the part of society and none from the government. When Junaid Khan was killed on a crowded railway platform, no one came to his aid, and later there were no witnesses, everyone claimed to have been somewhere else, or busy with something so consuming that the cries of a man being butchered and his brothers did not reach them. Examine the damage that was done: two men died, in terror and unimaginable pain. If that does not matter to us, do we think of those who killed and will not be punished? How many were they? Eight? Ten? Twenty? We don't know, we make no effort to know. Those men, they must have gone home after they killed. What food did they eat that evening? Who cooked it for them? How many greeted them in their mohallas the next morning? There are eight, ten, twenty murderers roaming freely in our society. In another year there may be eight hundred, or twenty thousand. Murder will be normal then. It will be like any other job—like weaving a beautiful carpet or sari, driving a car, tending a garden, writing software or nursing the sick. Killers will emerge among us, kill and come back home after a day's work. They might be our children, our siblings, our husbands or wives. Have we agreed to this? When we cast our vote, was this the world we chose?

Let us not turn away from what is happening. The future is grim. Due to the ongoing poisonous Hindu-Muslim discourse, human bombs are being prepared in large numbers, out of hatred among the Hindus and out of sheer fear among the Muslims. Our society is poised to reach its nadir. In places with dense populations, communalism will incubate more human bombs.

There are many ways to falsify history. During the West Bengal elections of 2016, we saw new wonders of the national curriculum unfold. In no time at all the 'Netaji files' were exhumed from the central government archives and aired, and an impression was created that one of the icons of our freedom movement, Subhas Chandra Bose, had been denied his place in history until now and that he would now be given his due. It did not matter that almost every child in India knows of him, that he has found a prominent place in the national narrative and in textbooks across the country for decades, and his pictures have adorned millions of homes and offices. For days we heard of Netaji from his new champions—many of whom had never bothered with him before. Sometimes he was pitted against Nehru and at other times in opposition to other leaders. There was a chorus of concern for Netaji. but once the BJP lost the state election, he was consigned to oblivion.

This kind of misuse of history must be avoided at all cost. By all means, visit a library to know more about the ups and downs in the relationship between Nehru and Bose. However, if you look towards a television studio debate to learn more about their equation, be warned that numerous pitfalls await you—prime among them being an anchor who doesn't have the time to read two newspapers a day or a single book in an entire year but becomes a historian by night, destroying your mind on a daily basis.

This is not an issue that is limited to our times but concerns future generations as well. We have managed to come this far without much mishap. But how many will now fall into the many pits being dug all around in front of our eyes, I cannot say. What I *can* say is that it is not you and I alone who will fall into these traps; we will be condemned to seeing our children being ensnared and injured—the children we dandle on our laps, wishing them a bright future.

There are many new heroes who emerge these days, fully formed, with entire mythologies of physical bravery and success, and make a grand entry into politics, dressed to kill. They want to wipe out the past, rewrite it in their own image. They think they are creating history in the present, whereas history has scripted the present of the likes of them a long time ago. Try as they might, they cannot change it. They will be exposed, we only need to keep our eyes and ears open.

If we learn to negotiate the past, we will no longer be perplexed or fooled by the present. For instance, there was no need to invoke the name of Sardar Patel during the Gujarat elections of late 2017; his name had already been used during the Lok Sabha elections of 2014. Except that this time around his name was being used liberally to placate the disgruntled Patel community of the state. Did it work? We don't know. But I humbly submit to the Patel community: Sardar is too big a statesman to belong to one group, or to be dragged into the arena of cynical politics.

A narrative has been built about the animosity between Sardar Patel and Jawaharlal Nehru, the latter being the villain. But if the new heroes of our nation would care to listen, I would tell them: If you read the correspondence between Nehru and Sardar, and dispassionate records of their relationship, your eyes will well up. If such friends, such co-travellers were to become a part of your life, you would be blessed indeed. If you can be Nehru to someone and that person can be Patel to you, know that you have earned the world's most precious riches. But, if by your deeds you have repudiated the legacy of the very person you hail as Sardar, if you have appropriated him and reduced him to a 182-metre statue, you have lost everything.

Some forty-fifty years after Sardar Patel, we saw one more 'Sardar' come and go in Indian politics. In between, he rode a rath. He too was called 'lauh purush' (iron man), he too set out to control and transform India, but is not to be seen opening his mouth these days. History can be like that, too.

To come back to Nehru and Patel, the immense respect they had for each other and their friendship ought to be compulsory reading for those studying politics. How, in spite of differing viewpoints, they continued to respect each other, is what should be taught in classrooms, not that Nehru and Patel destroyed each other's lives and aspirations. No, it was not so. In Indian politics there cannot be a bigger example of two statesmen, two individuals, forging a path of accord in the midst of differences.

An attempt is being made to erase that history. But the attempt will not succeed for the simple reason that someone has lived that history. How can that which has been lived be obliterated?

The above-mentioned instances are not mere tactics of one-upmanship in the battle between two political parties. They are part of a careful strategy to exert control over us—to seize and occupy our minds. For, when we start looking at the present and the past with their gaze, we will no longer be ourselves. Slowly but surely we are being moulded into a people who can be easily controlled by means of routine mechanisms of authority—a lapdog media, biased text books, IT cells, the Aadhar number...

Organizations based on caste, religion and intolerant politics are increasing their stranglehold on history. Tearing down a few posters, ransacking libraries and cinema halls suffices for leaders of these organizations to become historians. Burning history books presents a way of becoming a part of history, as does the act of filing an FIR against a writer. Most of all, if you know the way to the neighbourhood of the person you have been taught to see as the 'other', and if you walk there with flashing eyes and even a stick in your hand, you are a part of history and a historian.

This wonder of wonders can only be accomplished in

India, not in other places. In other countries, you have to spend five to ten years of your life researching one tiny part of one particular subject before you earn the right to be called a historian. In this new and restless India, however, anyone who shreds a few posters at the crossroads becomes a historian.

One is always a little anxious these days—anyone with the desire to become a historian bubbling inside him can take offence. The rich and the powerful, politicians and industrialists alike, have even thinner skins. Many well-wishers advise me to be careful with my words. I often forget their advice. But I haven't yet said anything that would prompt an advocate or attorney general to take a day off to file a case, feeling the urgent need to get a gag order against me. I'm certainly not going to speak about those who grow their revenue 16,000-fold in a single year—who knows, I might end up losing 16,000 times the amount I'm likely to earn in this lifetime! So I usually try to ensure no big fish suffers a loss of reputation by what I say, and I do not suffer a loss of such wealth as I shall never own.

If any of the big fish still want to file a defamation suit against me, I have a small request to make: please do not slap a lawsuit of Rs 100 crore on me. By all means file a suit, but let it be in the range of sawa rupaya—one and a quarter rupee—after all, an offering of sawa rupaya is enough to please our gods. I am imagining an India where nobody will suffer a loss of reputation worth more than sawa rupaya. Even if the oceanic gap between the poor and the rich becomes wider, like the chasm between two rotis and twenty cakes, let there be no disparity in the matter of measuring loss of reputation. May there be one measure of defamation for everybody, namely sawa rupaya. The work of lawyers will become much easier and the law minister too will get an opportunity to attend to some other work.

In the interest of democracy and freedom, I have coined a slogan:

One reputation, one loss
One nation, one reputation
Sawa rupaya respect for all!

It is very feudal, this law of defamation. The powerful and the rich have begun to make liberal use of this law. Have you ever heard of the poor claim that their reputation has been damaged? Have you heard any poor man say, 'You have not given me the minimum support price. You have brought me to a point where, out of sheer remorse that I have not been able to pay off my loans, I can only commit suicide. So I am going to hang myself. You are responsible for the great shame of reneging on my loan and not being able to look after my family. I will file a suit against you for causing a loss of reputation'? But the rich and the powerful use the law of defamation without compunction to intimidate us, the citizens. It is a law which reduces the status of the people in a democracy.

First the powerful lot intimidate us through their use of history. Then they use the law of defamation to do the same. This latter tactic has a particular advantage—no revealing light will ever reach those dark corners which hide secrets, because how many have the strength to withstand the threat of a Rs 100 crore defamation suit?

As it is, big corporates use this law to keep themselves out of the media's reach. Practically no one speaks out against them. If you email them detailing the charges levelled against them and ask them for a response, there is none forthcoming. What does come your way is a legal notice from them.

It is exactly this immunity from any legitimate questions that political parties are now seeking for themselves. The hurt caused to the reputation and prestige of those in power seems to be so severe that they feel the need to file defamation suits on any and every little matter. And they call themselves the guiding lights of democracy! This is nothing but a design to wear the people out so that they remain powerless against the cozy relationship building up between the mainstream media, big corporate houses and politicians.

Recently, Rajasthan came perilously close to enacting a law—the proposed Criminal Laws (Rajasthan Amendment) Bill, 2017—to stop anyone from reporting on corruption charges against public servants, magistrates and judges. Fortunately, the citizens and journalists of the state rose in protest—had they not spoken out now, they would never have been able to speak. The *Rajasthan Patrika*, especially, took a courageous stand, with the editor Gulab Kothari saying his piece immediately in a front-page editorial that minced no words—his paper would boycott the chief minister until she revoked the ordinance. Some days later, Gulab Kothari left the editorial column blank. It was a powerful symbolic act, for it carried echoes of the Emergency. The reason we should be vigilant on hearing these echoes anywhere is simple: the Emergency was a dark phase in our history and should never be repeated. If that period were to be repeated, as sometimes seems likely, then this time around our essence and consciousness of being the people will be completely erased.

The power of the people is being eroded not just

in India but around the world. Hundreds of journalists have been sent to prison—not just in countries like China and Saudi Arabia which have a long history of persecuting journalists, but also in Russia, Turkey, Israel, Egypt, Philippines, Argentina, Ukraine, Mexico, the United States, as governments are increasingly establishing their control over the world of communication. That was exactly what the Rajasthan government tried to do. Had the law been enacted, journalists would have virtually become bonded labour. It is the age of the lapdog media in any case; most media organizations have jumped happily into the lap of power. However, the system is ruthless; it can choke the eager-to-please child without missing a beat.

In our democracy today, the political system overwhelmingly dominates the citizen; our power is weakening. Consequently, while leaders are being elevated to the position of veritable avatars, the people are being relegated to the category of criminals. If you pose a question, you are branded an anti-national and taken to task—how dare you question the avatar-purush, the incarnation of the mightiest god? Campaigns are unleashed against you on social media and you are virtually encircled and trolled. In the process, you start becoming fearful, telling your children they are far too visible on Facebook, that they should be less vocal. So, bit by bit, we surrender the little space we occupy as citizens. The more we cede that space, the more we enfeeble ourselves. It is not desirable for everybody to support one political party or ideology. It is important to have a plurality of parties and ideologies and we as the people should have the confidence that we can deal with it.

Essential to the idea of democracy is an understanding of being the people and staking our claim to democracy. However, when people's consciousness transforms into people's fear, they become mere servants. In a democracy, the people come first in all senses; the system is meant to serve them, be answerable to them. What the powers that be are seeking to do is to invert that order so that the system dominates us. Their ultimate aim is to ensure that we swallow any mumbo-jumbo they direct at us. Their aim is perpetual, untrammeled power.

To this end they are engaged in unnerving us with acrimonious debates day after day so that our daily diet of bellicose TV makes us wonder if there is an all-out war between communities out there, which leads to a deepening mutual suspicion and rancour in society. It also homogenizes society, forces everyone into the same mould, so anyone who is different—who dresses a little differently, has a different diet, raises a different slogan, worships a different god—is marked. And so we are silenced.

To prevent anybody from speaking is a form of terrorism, too. To create an atmosphere of fear and suspicion is also a form of terrorism.

In recent times a new trend has emerged among citizens. Putting their unqualified trust in the leader they submerge themselves and their aspirations in him completely. This is not a good thing. When a voter merges in the leader, he is no longer the people, or even a voter. He is merely the dust swept up by a windstorm.

The power that resides in the people must not be frittered away. Be a film star's fan, or cricketer's, but never be a politician's fan. Respect him, but don't be so hypnotized by his words that you forget to evaluate his work and hold him to the promises he makes. You did not elect him or her to make stunning speeches. Your mandate was for social and economic well-being. Your loyalty, on a personal level, can be towards any leader and any political party. There is also no problem at all if you are a party worker. But as long as you consider yourself a citizen of the country, your conduct should be that of a citizen's. The task of demanding answers, with impartiality and without prejudice, is yours, and overrides any obligation to an organization. If you behave like the agent of a political party or a religious or cultural organization, you will destroy this democracy. It is your responsibility that after you vote a party into power, you step back and become impartial once more. If you think something is right, and good, call it so; and if something is wrong, call it wrong, too.

We are already suffering the consequences that follow the erosion of our status as citizens, for which we, too, must share the blame. We are living in a perpetual state of uncertainty, wondering about the safe limits within which we can air our differences with authority, without 'becoming' or being branded a dissenter. It has become a pattern that the person one is talking to is invariably at pains to clarify, *no*, I am *not* a dissenter. My response to that is, so what if you are? I understand if you say you are not krodhi (resentful), I respect that, but why feel ashamed of calling yourself a virodhi (dissenter)? Is it written anywhere in our shastras that having an opposing point of view is prohibited? Truth be told, if you say you are *not* an objector, you are ranged against democracy. If you have a different point of view, *say* you are a dissenter. Post ten things on Facebook daily and say openly, 'Yes, I have a difference of opinion.' Being an objector is no crime.

If we are not vigilant about our rights in a democracy,

it does not matter how much Bournvita and Chyavanprash we consume. It is time to stop looking for all sorts of excuses for our 'lack of strength', or powerlessness, and face the reality that this enfeeblement of citizens has come about because we have abandoned dissent and turned to supplication. There's a world of difference between the two. The process of supplication is quite similar to the act of propitiation typical of a bhakt, a devotee—the gods are angry, they need to be placated; they are bound to hear us eventually, all we have to do is draw their attention towards us.

Take the trader-business fraternity of Surat which kept up its demonstrations against demonetization and GST for almost six months in 2017, suffering considerable economic losses in the process. I observed them quite closely. Whenever and wherever they came out to demonstrate, their numbers were impressive. However, and this is the interesting bit, instead of protesting, they were adopting a posture of entreaty. The Surat traders were putting forward their demands as devotees sing Sai bhajans, in full rhyme. Nowhere were any slogans raised. Cries of 'zindabad', 'murdabad', 'ho barbaad' are so commonplace in a democracy that they are hurled at politicians all the time, without a moment's hesitation. But no such slogans were heard in the markets and streets of

Surat. Only the number of bodies suggested there was a kind of protest going on. When we no longer remain the people, we are reduced to being just numbers. The movement had no impact whatsoever.

The way the traders saw it, their movement failed because the Union finance minister did not pay heed to their demands. In reality, their inability to see themselves as citizens was the sole reason for their campaign's failure.

Some time ago in Delhi I received a phone call from a lady who told me that alarmed by the rising levels of pollution in the city she had been spurred into action. Now she wanted me to highlight the issue of pollution in my show and mention her work as well. She was convinced that if ten or fifteen television news channels highlighted her endeavour, which involved school children as well, it would have an impact. I pointed out to her that the serious problem of pollution was receiving steady coverage already. If her efforts were not having the desired impact, she needed to re-examine her approach. The lady thought I was a pessimist. I urged her to continue her efforts and never give up, to which she said, 'We are protesting so hard. All I want is to draw the attention of the prime minister.'

So there it was again—entreaty; supplication. Sing bhajans at the supreme leader's door till he turns his attention to you, if at all, and deigns to solve your problem, if he can at all. Approach the prime minister as a citizen, I wanted to tell her. If it is a bhakt you want to be, there is an elaborate system of crores of gods and goddesses in the Hindu religion. If perchance you are unable to locate the nearest deity, worship a tree. Hinduism can be liberal that way.

Finally, I wrote the lady a letter:

> *What you are doing is neither inadequate nor wrong. In fact, you are doing more than your share. Not just you, many people who are worked up about various issues are engaged in similar efforts. Their questions are valid too, for they are about life and death issues. But none of these efforts is having any impact. The list of unproductive movements by citizens is becoming longer by the day and even if several more were to be added to this list it would make no difference to the system or ministers or the government. In a couple of instances, they may even agree to some demands, but after a point no progress is ever made. For the last four years Delhi has been in the grip of a serious health hazard—from small children to the elderly, everyone is at risk and their lungs are getting damaged. This is an issue by itself; it does not have to be made into one.*

Ma'am, all this is happening because the real power of 'the people' is no longer yours. If as a fan or blind supporter you—like so many others—have unreservedly put your entire trust in a leader after the election, then you are no longer the citizen of a democracy. When you forsake that mantle to don the mask of the leader, sport his tattoo on your cheek, merge in him and become his reflection, the power you wield as the people goes. This is why you, and others, find it difficult to understand why your efforts are not making any headway whatsoever—in the last four or five years Delhi's air quality has gone from bad to hazardous, yet no movement has made the slightest difference. The ideology and reflection of the leader is lodged within you and as long as you don't make any efforts to separate yourself from that persona, you will not become part of the people. That is why you are not being able to grasp the reason for your lack of impact.

Farmers face bullets, they hang themselves—does it affect you? Every day in every state farmers are facing ruin—has it roused you to action? College after college is devoid of teachers—do you really care? When we as the people do not support our own, do not care about their problems, how will our words about anything have any impact? Just as you were silent in someone's hour of need, so someone is silent in your time of need. Therefore,

I say, exercise your right to speak out. If others speak for their rights, add your voice to theirs. You become the people only when you speak out and express solidarity. Whenever others raise their voice, encourage them. Even if you do not always agree with their endeavour, support them to the extent that they are able to speak and others are able to hear them out.

Each one of us is fighting a lone battle today. It is proving difficult to extend any struggle beyond a certain limit. Citizens are betraying fellow citizens. As for the system, deviousness is an inherent part of its make-up. And by not assuming the status of the people we are just making its task easier. What is novel is the way in which the system is pinning you down in a Hindu-Muslim framework. Pehlu Khan, Akhlaq and Junaid, who were killed, were not Muslims; they were citizens. In Kerala, when RSS workers are killed and CPM workers are killed in retaliation, and vice versa, those who die are not Hindus or Communists but citizens. Therefore, speak out; support your fellow citizens. Any extreme manifestation of politics thrives on division and distrust in society, it ultimately diminishes the citizens, depriving them of the essence and consciousness of being the people.

It is for these reasons I say, ma'am, your effort is honest but ineffective.

Sure enough, Delhi's media soon shifted its focus to the issue of Rani Padmavati, who may or may not have existed, and a film made on her story. Gasping five- and eighty-five-year-olds were forgotten. It was back to manufacturing history, demonizing the Muslim and celebrating Hindu valour, for which women must burn.

The Hindu-Muslim framework has become the sole benchmark for any and every issue. Bogus nationalism is another. These frameworks have become so entrenched that it is not going to be an easy task to extricate ourselves from them; we will have to work very hard at it. We think being the people in a democracy is a breeze. On the contrary, it takes more hard work than is required to get through an IIT entrance exam. We do not become the people so easily or for free. The manner in which our youth are being seduced into a life of materialistic enslavement, they will be reduced to being mere cogs in the system for the next twenty to twenty-five years. Perhaps fifty. They will not be the people any more. India will not be a democracy.

Power has a hundred ways to terrorize people. The easiest way is to slap a case of sedition against you, or to arrest you for saying, writing or—increasingly now—sharing anything deemed 'objectionable'. This is happening across India, in state after state. It has become an epidemic since the present government came to power, but the trend is neither new, nor exclusive to the BJP. Duly elected governments have been making the ordinary citizen defenceless for some years now, from Tamil Nadu to Uttar Pradesh. First they pit the crowd against you, then the police and lawyers, and finally they show you the door that opens into a prison.

During the freedom struggle one of Gandhiji's biggest contributions was to wipe away the fear of British prisons from the minds of the weakest Indians. To keep the fear of prison alive, the British constructed the Cellular Jail in the Andaman's—Kaala Paani, the terrible prison in the black waters. But Gandhi had so ended the fear of prisons that people were not intimidated, and went there too. Some of them apologized to the British authorities, pleading to be released, but I won't dismiss their claim to being revolutionaries. Prisons are like that—they can break your spirit. Our governments today know this well.

Therefore, I say, just as there is a provision of anticipatory bail, there should be a provision of anticipatory jail. Then one can voluntarily petition the court: 'My lords, since I have an apprehension, and summer vacations are round the corner, I would like to spend the next two months in jail. Later, if the government foists a false case upon me, please subtract the duration already spent in jail from the term given.'

Till now many of us have abstained from speaking out because we are afraid it could land us in prison. How about starting a campaign: 'On such and such date we would like to go to prison, just like that. Let us all pack our lunch-boxes with a couple of dry paranthas to last us a couple of days each and spend two or three days in jail so that the fear of false cases and prison terms entrenched in society is uprooted. Down with fear!'

If we consider ourselves followers of Gandhi, we must ask for the introduction of a provision of anticipatory jail so that we liberate ourselves from the yoke of fear.

Is my suggestion too radical? Am I losing my bearings? If you think I am, let me share with you just a short list of cases. It might seem a bit boring but bear with me. You will remember most of these cases, you will have heard of them, but reading them together is instructive. It puts things in perspective.

- In April 2012, a professor was arrested in West Bengal because he posted a cartoon that critiqued the chief minister, Mamata Banerjee.
- In May 2012, two Air India employees were

arrested for objectionable posts against the then prime minister Manmohan Singh.

- In November 2012, two girls, Shaheen and Renu, were arrested for their posts on social media questioning the way Mumbai was brought to a standstill on the day of Shiv Sena chief Bal Thackeray's funeral.
- In May 2014, a man was booked in Goa for posting a Facebook comment critical of the newly elected prime minister, Narendra Modi. (The charge against him: 'promoting communal and social disharmony'. Politicians and television news anchors who do exactly this day in and day out are never booked or interrogated.)
- In March 2015, a student of Class XI was arrested in UP for commenting against Azam Khan, a senior leader of the Samajwadi Party which was in power at the time.
- In November 2016, a nineteen-year-old RTI activist was arrested in Madhya Pradesh for a post criticizing the prime minister and the state's chief minister for demonetization.
- In March 2017, seven people were arrested in UP, within hours of Yogi Adityanath's swearing in as chief minister, for 'objectionable' posts about him.

- In May, 2017, Karnataka police arrested two youths for putting up a post with a morphed picture of PM Modi which, according to the complainant—no relation of the PM himself—made him look 'obscene and ugly'. (Soon after this, the administration in far-off Varanasi, the prime minister's constituency, issued a notice that people sharing rumours or falsehoods would be arrested. The falsehoods about India's first prime minister, Nehru, have resulted in no arrests. Not long ago, Amit Malviya, of the BJP's IT cell, posted a tweet about Nehru hugging several women. Since when has hugging a woman become a bad thing? It turned out that one of the women was Nehru's sister, the other his niece.)
- In October 2017, cases were filed against twenty-two businessmen in Kanpur, of whom one was arrested. Their crime: putting the image of their prime minister alongside that of North Korea's supposedly lunatic Supreme Leader Kim Jong-un.
- In October 2017, a fan of the Tamil film star Vijay was arrested for making 'derogatory comments' against PM Modi.
- In October 2017, again, eighteen-year-old Zakir Ali Tyagi was imprisoned in UP for forty-two days,

alongside hardened criminals, for a Facebook post where he made light of a court order that had declared the Ganga a 'legal entity' and called the BJP government's promise to build a Ram mandir a gimmick.

- In December 2018, Manipuri journalist Kishorechandra Wangkhemcha was jailed under the National Security Act (NSA) for criticizing the BJP governments in Manipur and the Centre.
- In January 2019, Tamil politician Sathiyaraj Balu was arrested for lampooning Narendra Modi on Facebook, and in May, BJP activist Priyanka Sharma was arrested in Bengal for posting a caricature of Mamata Banerjee.

This is only a short list. In the course of their political careers, politicians face a great deal of criticism. Their opponents denigrate them to their face, not even behind their backs, and in the choicest of language. They don't arrest one another for these insults. Invariably, it is someone from among us that the police come for.

As per my count, from 2014 till late 2017, forty-two citizens had either been arrested or had cases filed against them for making objectionable remarks about the prime minister or any BJP chief minister or leader. The number of Muslims was the highest, but there were Hindus on the list, too, and Sikhs and Christians. Every one of them was a citizen. That is what we need to understand.

The process of being democratic requires great courage. It requires constant practice. Duck 'net practice' for a day and your ability to be democratic will be diminished. And in the new India, there are many distractions that keep us away from this necessary practice.

From the time privatization gathered pace in India, leading to a corporate culture, people from the corporate world have almost completely disappeared from democratic participation. There are very few exceptions. Scarcely anybody ventures out of his or her firm. It's as if anybody who enters the corporate world is out of the democratic set-up, leading a lifestyle that prompts him or her to value democracy less and less. They start imagining India can only be saved by a dictatorship—naturally, a market-friendly dictatorship.

Although privatization was presented as the answer to many of democracy's ills, it has enfeebled the very idea of democracy. The corporate world has not provided a fillip to democratic participation because it has formed a nexus with the political class, and they are working together against the interests of the people. The political system enervates citizens at one end and the corporates keep citizens away from actively participating in democracy at the other end. Then together they can do as they please—acquire land here, raze a mountain there, create a situation where farmers are driven to digging holes and standing in them for weeks to demand a fair price for their land, but to no avail.

The more privatization increases, the more democratic spaces shrink. Corporates have never had any interest in democracy. But we don't examine the link between governments and corporations, we don't question it. We don't protest the electoral bonds scheme introduced by the government that will turn political donations completely opaque, making it easier for big business to capture the electoral process and impossible for the public to know how and to what extent government policies are tailored to benefit the big donors.

There is a lot that we don't question, a lot that we just don't see.

In December 2017, the winter session of the Lok Sabha, the country's highest legislative body, was postponed because of the high-stakes Gujarat Assembly elections where Prime Minister Modi was scheduled to campaign extensively. The nation's business was made subordinate to a state election. There was some debate about this in the papers, almost none on television. But how many of us really demanded an explanation? After all, in this age of social media it is possible to launch campaigns and make a lot of noise.

Even those of us who raised the issue of the Lok Sabha session being delayed did not notice a larger trend. For the last thirty years, the number of Vidhan Sabha sessions has dwindled alarmingly in state after state. Consequently, the significance of Assembly sessions in the running of a state government has reduced steadily. The Assembly is the platform where MLAs discuss issues relating to their constituencies and thus evolve into leaders. Today, if MLAs are not ministers, nobody knows them. They do their own thing, winning and losing elections, but are of little use to the people who elect them.

We have stopped looking at these institutions. We don't bother to ask why a state's chief minister or the prime minister chooses not to hold an Assembly or Lok Sabha session at the designated time or merely goes through the motions. Is it that we no longer have any confidence in the Vidhan Sabha or the Lok Sabha? I refuse to believe that. If we did not have confidence in these institutions, seventy per cent or more among us would not be exercising our vote in election after election. I think the problem is that we have reduced our chief democratic right, and chief responsibility, to merely the act of pressing a button on the voting machine. Then we return from the polling station and submerge ourselves in the image of the leader who emerges victorious.

To have faith is a good thing, no doubt. But that faith should rest on the foundation of facts, not emotions.

In late 2017, the Pew Research Center, an American think tank, released the results of a survey it had conducted in India during the first quarter of that year. The survey had been conducted among 2,464 people across India's most populous states. (Yes, 2,464 persons. It is an intriguing figure, even forgetting that the country they were surveying is home to well over a billion people. Why not add another thirty-six people and make it 2,500, at least? Perhaps they had an astrologer advising them.)

The survey found that 88 per cent of the respondents held a favourable opinion of Narendra Modi as prime minister—'almost nine out of every ten', said the survey. This in itself isn't new or startling; some other surveys of the time had reported similar results. It is the replies to other questions that are cause for great concern.

To be honest, I was also worried for the tenth respondent in every batch of ten who did not find the prime minister the most popular leader. I felt like telling him, bhai, when nine respondents have gone one way, why are you standing alone on the other side? Then it struck me: this one man is the real democrat. By standing alone, away from the others, he was in fact doing a great service to Indian democracy. Otherwise, out of sheer anxiety that nine out of ten had gone over to one side, he could have decided to cross over, too, for a perfect ten! But he stood his ground. Whoever he is, I salute him. He has kept the prestige of democracy intact—standing apart and standing firm to ensure the leader had at least one opponent.

Predictably, the 88 per cent popularity rating for the Supreme Leader among 2,464 people led to celebrations on Twitter. I wondered if the people who were in raptures had read the entire findings of the survey. Fifty-three per cent of the respondents favoured military rule in the country. Nine out of ten respondents put their faith in an individual who has come up through a democratic process; an individual who is by virtue of his political career a symbol of democratic aspirations, ascending from the position of chief minister to that of prime minister. Then why did five out of the nine who supported him favour military rule? Didn't they have full faith in the elected leader they hailed as the most popular?

The respondents would have been asked one question:

'Do you think military rule is good?' Over half of them would have said yes. I would have asked them a second question: 'Would you support a military rule where someone knocks on your door at two in the night and whisks you and your father away and locks you up in a dungeon for ten years without recourse to any lawyer or defence?' Would the same respondents have answered yes to that question? I don't think so.

And what name would they have given had they been asked who should lead that military regime? Would they have named a democratically elected leader? Would they have named the former Army chief who is now a minister? That would have been logical, after all.

Just how muddled are we on the subject of democracy and the leader? Why are we so confused? Our confusion arises from the fact that the daily practice of democracy that happened in our institutions, be it in the media or any other institution, has become a thing of the past. Those daily 'practice matches' of analysis and interrogation are long gone. If we think the blame for this decline can be laid only at the door of the present government, we would be mistaken. It would mean we haven't quite understood the age we are in. This deterioration has taken place over the last twenty-five to thirty years, as hyper capitalism and its technologies have taken over our lives, as inequality has grown dramatically and demagogues have risen, and as institutions have been systematically dismantled or hollowed out. We may feel it more now only because the proportion of those who are alert to institutional erosion is greater today because it is happening at great speed.

The Pew survey also had 55 per cent of the respondents saying they wanted a 'strong leader', one who could 'make decisions without interference from parliament or the courts'. The survey report noted that 'support for autocratic rule is higher in India than in any other nation surveyed.'

Why is a strong leader required? Is the framework of Constitutional laws and powers given to a leader or chief minister so inadequate that a muscleman is needed in that position? Does the supreme leader have to wrestle with the cabinet secretary, administer some well-placed blows? Why this yearning for a strong leader, then? It would be understandable if the desire was for a leader who represents the strong will of the people. Perhaps it was. But do the kind of questions that are asked in these surveys allow for nuance? Do those who celebrate the results of such surveys have any time for nuance?

On the one hand there is a mythical narrative of a strong elected leader being created, and running parallel to it is a script for military rule. There might be a reason.

Until now our democratic institutions, even when functioning at their best, have roundly failed to fulfil the aspirations of the people. On the contrary, through these institutions, the control of vested interests on public resources and systems has become near complete. It is true not only of India but of countries the world over that one or two per cent of the population controls ninety to ninety-five per cent of the nation's wealth. This information has not emerged from some communist party office; it is based on surveys by economists who believe in the capitalist system. For instance, the figure of one or two per cent controlling almost the entire wealth of some nations is from a report by OXFAM.

And this is what is making the political class nervous. Of the ninety per cent or more of the population who are hard put to feed themselves, some are committing suicide for now. But the day they tire of taking their lives, they will rise in revolt. There are limits to dying, and there are limits to killing too. History is replete with the names of murderous tyrants; even so, in the end it was they who perished, not humanity.

This is the politician's biggest anxiety. Whoever holds the reins of power is haunted by this fear. Tomorrow if some among us happen to be in power, the same fear will plague us. It is a legitimate fear, for politicians have nothing to show other than the same old formula of propaganda and event management. Democracy can be difficult to manage. This explains the dramatics of creating a halo around the idea of autocratic or military rule through strategic questions in regular surveys, because it is the easiest way to trample on the expectations and aspirations of the people, by co-opting them into the project of their own disenfranchisement. When we relinquish our standing as citizens, one day we will wake up to find a gunman standing outside our door and for the next ten or twenty years we will lapse into silence, losing our power of speech and our language.

It is to this end that both the narratives of the strong leader and of military rule are being lovingly nurtured, even though both of them are among the most clichéd narratives, or formulae, of history. Those who have not delved into history will also grasp it. Those who have studied history will grasp it better. And even those who go around tearing posters will understand this formula if they stop to think.

If it is a strong leader we desire, how would we describe Gandhi, Mandela, Lincoln, Martin Luther King and Vinoba Bhave? Strong leaders, wouldn't you say? The man with the frail frame who wore nothing but a dhoti and challenged the might of the British Empire—was he a weak or a strong leader? A strong leader does not necessarily have to be dressed to the hilt and thunder from a high stage; a half-naked, soft-spoken fakir can also be a strong leader. There shouldn't be an iota of confusion in our minds about this. A half-naked fakir too can be a strong leader who, armed with a sense of purpose, set out with his lathi and in thirty years removed the fear of the Cellular Jail, Kaala Paani, embedded deep in the minds of the people, inspiring them to stand up to British might. It speaks of his courage and the strength of his conviction that a Bhagat Singh, a Chandrashekhar Azad and a Bose emerged from the same stream. That is why I say a strong leader does not always come in colourful bandis. A strong leader does not emerge when you fight over God one week and start building temples to Gandhi's assassin, Godse, the next.

From 1940 to 1945, during the Second World War, the British prime minister, Winston Churchill, was incredibly popular—he continues to be quoted to this day—and people believed everything he said. He seemed to be the world's biggest leader of the time; people were hanging on his every word in the belief that anything he said went a long way. He commanded blind faith. After the war, when elections were held, the same Churchill suffered a defeat at the hands of Clement Attlee. A strong leader also suffers defeat.

Living in a democracy, if we dilute our understanding of what it means to be the people, we will be betraying our freedom struggle. We give pensions to our freedom fighters, but how many of them do we know, those unnamed lovers of freedom who spent years in prison? Their children and their children's children faced ruin across generations; relying solely on those meagre pensions they inexorably slid into penury. Those freedom fighters staked the futures of several generations of their families to win the right to be citizens of an independent nation. In honour of their memory, at least, we must not lose the essence of our great democracy and the right to be its people.

As for the narrative of the strong leader, it is a kind of time-pass, nothing more. He who takes everybody along is a leader, not one with a trail of people walking behind him. There were many tall leaders around Gandhi—Rajendra Prasad, Ambedkar, Nehru, Bose, Sardar Patel and many more. It is that which creates conditions for a true democracy. Where one leader dwarfs the landscape, there will be no *lok*, only *tantra*, no people, only a hollowed-out system, and the only thing left standing will be a temple of falsehood. We owe it to ourselves to rebuild our democratic consciousness and reclaim our right to be the people.

The Babas of India Are Here to Stay

Frequently, at the beginning of women's periods, a situation arises in which bleeding starts when they are in their houses' most pure and sacred locations. Generally those areas which are forbidden—like the kitchen while cooking, or the puja room while cleaning it, or some other similar pure place where women are not meant to be at that time of the month. In the first days of the bleeding one doesn't lay a hand on anything in the kitchen at all but this is a cycle which happens every month, and it isn't in your hands at all. So if any such incident has happened to you during the entire year, there is one day to deliver you from your 'paap bodh', your sense of sin, the day of the Rishi Panchami…

The video in which I heard this statement being made by a baba was featured on one of the top three Hindi news channels on television. I watched the video and others featuring the baba on YouTube. The name of the news channel isn't important here because all news channels on television and websites in all languages, with the exception of NDTV India, feature programmes like these—from horoscopes to 'instructional' videos like the one I watched. My intention is to examine what is said on these programmes, what has changed in them over time, and the vexations of our age which they reflect. I am trying to understand the scriptural knowledge quoted and recommended by Baba—the sage in the YouTube video—through the eyes of those women who are trying to break the many pre-conceived notions about periods and menstruation.

On the surface, it is easy to see how the colourful babas who feature on these news channels are digging out old superstitions and re-establishing them in modern contexts. Yet they are shrewd and intelligent too. They aren't among us to foment revolution, to go back into the past and reclaim the 'golden age of yoga or ayurved'; rather, these babas are master salesmen who are peddling a single cure for the one hundred and eight ills which afflict human beings—and, in the process, building their personal financial empires. Thus, single-minded devotion to tradition will not serve their purpose, and so these babas give as generous a space to modernity as they do to those nonsensical ideas within modernity which masquerade as tradition. More on this later.

The critics of television have focused all their energies

on the ills which affect prime-time news programmes that are broadcast in the evening. A major strand in these programmes is the question of women's 'security' and what can be done to 'liberate' women within our city-spaces. What has escaped most of these critics is the crowd of these influential astrologer-anchors who populate the morning prime-time segments, in their clothes and demeanour that are customized for the occasion, and come together to reinforce and exploit the insecurities of such a large section of society, especially women.

The question of whether astrology is itself valid or invalid is now past debate. Barring one or two people, I don't know anyone who doesn't consult an astrologer as routinely as they would a doctor. It clearly has an iron grip.

In comparison to babas who broadcast in Hindi, those who do so in English are a class apart. In place of daily horoscopes, they peddle life-management pills to harried customers. Interviews with English-speaking babas are conducted very respectfully and the English-speaking babas look upon Hindi-speaking ones with contempt. When a poor person takes refuge with a baba for the sake of spiritualism, it becomes superstition; when the rich take refuge with their babas for the sake of spiritualism, it becomes a stress-management course.

After Gurmeet Ram Rahim Singh Insan, the head of the Dera Sacha Sauda of Sirsa, Haryana, was sent to jail after being convicted on two counts of rape, it was written in many places that it is only poor people who come under the influence of babas. That's nonsense. Rich people and the middle class have thrown up babas like Gurmeet too. The only difference is that they speak in English and peddle aloe vera juice.

In contemporary India, political leaders and ministers conduct secret pujas which cost lakhs of rupees. No one talks about this expenditure which remains unrecorded either by PAN cards or Aadhaar numbers. Our political class is the biggest guardian of superstition. From cricketers to distinguished members of society, everyone is a guardian of blind belief. So no one should call the supporters of Ram Rahim's Dera in Sirsa an army of ignorants.

It is nonsense, too, to say that news channels are responsible for the birth and proliferation of babas. It would be more correct to say that babas have their own channels via which they communicate with the public. There are many other information channels too on which newer varieties of babas keep rising. Babas have their own websites and social media teams. And all babas are astrologers, and vice versa, which gives them many other platforms. There is fierce competition among the astrology programmes on Hindi channels. Each programme is a brand in its own right.

But to come back to the YouTube video and Baba who dispensed advice to menstruating women. Many of the episodes of that particular programme which Baba hosts carry the tagline: 'Find out how to get money that will last seven lifetimes.' Crores of Indians live their entire lives below the poverty line. Those above the line too struggle as hard. To tell them that they will receive money that will last seven lifetimes is not rocket science—who will not be tempted to watch?

On his show, Baba claimed that if one keeps a regular fast of sixteen days over sixteen years for the goddess Mahalakshmi, one will gain an uninterrupted supply of wealth. This was a fast he too kept during his hard times, he said. What I couldn't understand was whether uninterrupted wealth came into his life after the coming of television or because he kept the fast. He described rich people, saying that they behave in this way, or that way, and still they are prosperous. Then, deftly avoiding calling rich people corrupt, he said that they must have kept the fast for Mahalakshmi in one of their births because of which they had become prosperous in their present life. It was obvious that Baba knew how most of the rich and the prosperous become so in this country and, after all, everyone has an eye on the benefits which can accrue from such people.

What I liked was that while announcing the daily forecast, Baba mentioned, first of all, a suitable time for men and women to 'propose' to the opposite sex. He understood that given the traditions and culture in which people of this country have been kept entangled, they should be given allowances to love, and so he used those same traditions to declare the best time to 'propose'. In many of the videos, the suitable time was 5 a.m. So if anyone wanted to make a declaration of their love, they had better set an alarm before going off to sleep.

Baba had also coined a new word: 'lovemate'. This word is very different and modern from ancient-sounding words like 'Romeo' and 'love jihad'. Baba frequently used the word in the singular. From the word lovemate it would seem that he was talking about two people, but it turned out that Baba was talking about just one lovemate per sun sign. Baba never recommended that a Leo should go here or there for an assignation with his Sagittarian lovemate. What he did issue instructions on was when lovemates should visit temples, when they should feed Brahmins and priests, and when they should serve the elderly. In our society, lovers who choose each other on their own are looked upon as being against prevalent culture, as a pair who do not heed their parents' wishes. Baba rechristened these pairs lovemates and not only recommended them auspicious times for love but also instructed them to serve their parents, neatly pairing modernity with tradition.

I liked this word lovemate. Now, at the very least, what canoodling pairs can do when seized by the anti-Romeo squads out to stop men and women from coming together in public, is to tell them, 'We are lovemates. Baba on TV instructed us, and so we're here to serve the elderly. Let go of your batons, take this prasad and get lost.' But if the lovemates are only to serve the elderly, only god knows when they would find time to 'love' or to 'mate'!

On one show Baba told Piscean lovemates that they should tour places of religious significance that day. How I wished I could watch other shows hosted by Baba, to find out if he recommended that lovemates visit the cinema, or restaurants, or the Nehru, Lohia or Deendayal Parks. In one show he told Sagittarian lovemates that on that day they should take a bath and afterwards offer Datura to Lord Shiva. By doing so, their relationship would become even tenderer. I am convinced that Baba even tells lovemates when and how to shampoo their hair. In one episode, he told Leos that they could go out with their partners for a romantic dinner. I jumped with joy. See, I told myself, these babas on television cannot be against modernity. They know that their consumers will indeed go out on romantic dinners—even though romantic dinners are not part of the common cultural imagination in India. It was all one more excellent way of bringing modernity and tradition together, I thought, and an effective way to keep a toe in all waters.

Baba also recommended that Leos should eat vitamins to improve immunity. By Bajrang Bali, I swear that I heard this statement with my own ears and typed it with my own fingers. I didn't know that our great scriptures of astrology scriptures actually recommended antibiotics, and vitamins! Shut down our medical colleges! At the beginning of each show, he also gives out the most auspicious time to conduct a Caesarean Section—perhaps there's a huge market for auspicious times for Caesarean Sections. After all, each one wants a child in his or her own household who will go on to become famous so that every time they want a selfie, a ready celebrity can be found at home—who wants to rush off to an airport or a hotel each time? And on one episode, Baba advised Aquarian doctors to treat patients for free that day; doing so would give them professional success.

Baba also laid a great deal of stress on office politics, promotions and the like in his prognostications. From this, one can understand the limited and worthless context in which a common Indian views his office and workplace. Promotions, personal pride and ego seem to be the only acceptable categories. Then, on one episode, 'change in shift' was a new category that was added. He told Librans that their shift timings might change, and inconvenience them. But honestly, shifts change for employees in lakhs of offices throughout India. People have brought astrology even into this. He might say on one particular day that Geminis should keep their business plans secret. On the same day he might recommend to Sagittarians that a partnership in business might be beneficial to them. What I didn't understand was if, on that particular day, a Gemini could enter into a partnership with the Sagittarian for, after all, Baba had tipped the Gemini to keep his plans secret.

One day, Baba confused me. He declared that no auspicious task should be performed 12 minutes before and 12 minutes after 2.18 a.m. on 27 August. This is an inauspicious time, he warned. For a long time I kept thinking about who would be performing an auspicious task at this hour. Was Baba hinting at sex? No no, that couldn't be. And if something hasn't been clearly spelt out, why think along those lines at all? But who could be performing an auspicious task in the dead of the night, that too at 2.18 a.m.; what could that task be—I was thinking about all of this when Baba said that today, you should face in the southeasterly direction and take a pledge to free yourself from doubt and suspicion. Decide that you should not doubt, or suspect, at all. As soon as I took the pledge I was freed of the question of what that auspicious task might be which could not be performed 12 minutes before and 12 minutes after 2.18 a.m. on 27 August.

The category I found most important in his daily forecast was the 'Yayi Zayad Yog'. We all know that legal cases in India drag on for a long time. Not everyone has luck like Gurmeet Singh's, for whom a verdict arrived after fifteen long years. There are many who don't see verdicts arrive within their lifetimes and fall prey to injustice in the very exercise of seeking justice. There is no injustice in India greater than the process of filing and fighting legal cases. But Baba, under the aegis of the 'Yayi Zayad Yog', instructs when an application ought to be filed, when one should meet with a lawyer and when arguments should be put forward in court. Hardly any person making the rounds of the courts will not pause to listen to Baba recommending suitable times to visit the courts. If one can wait for hours at a bus stop to find transport to the courts, how hard is it to pause briefly in front of a television set? This is India, after all—a chief justice breaks down on camera and cries while asking for the number of judges in the judiciary to be increased. If judges themselves are weeping, how can litigants not? Baba saw an opportunity and expanded his market. On one episode, Baba instructed that the 'Yayi Zayad Yog' would fall that night between 8.10 p.m. and 12.37 a.m. I fell into a tizzy; the courts would be closed at that time! But Baba cleared my suspicion in the very next line when he said, 'I know courts remain closed at this time but you can go meet your lawyers. You can discuss your case with them.' Imagine: If the Yayi Zayad Yog was to fall between 12 a.m. and 5 a.m., lawyers would sleepwalk through their cases the following day.

Every day, astrology is expanding its sphere of influence to encompass all the myriad problems of Indian society. There is something special about India's Problems—what must have happened is that in some bygone age, these Problems must have drunk the special elixir of immortality and become eternal. They will never be solved, whether Manmohan Singh comes to power or Narendra Modi. Obviously, astrology is the only way to distract people from the Problems.

I am taken aback by the proliferation of these astrology programmes on television. Just as weather bulletins dominated by women anchors tell us the state of the weather in different cities across India, so do these programmes report the time when the evil influence of the planet Saturn will affect cities such as Delhi, Mumbai, Bhopal, Lucknow, Kolkata, Chandigarh and Ahmedabad. Why leave out Patna and Jaipur, I wonder. There are different fixed categories of what astrology will dictate how one's day will turn out—a grand day; a fantastic day; a good beginning is indicated; a normal day; a favourable day; a day that will bring golden moments; a day that will bring new gifts; a special day.

India is a country where people depend predominantly on astrology—just at the economy depends predominantly on agriculture. That is our reality. There are those who don't believe in astrology, sure, but they are so few in number that they probably know each other personally. Study those babas on television. A Gurmeet Singh does not become a Baba Ram Rahim only in Sirsa, he can become one anywhere in India. At any time. All that is needed is for someone to innovate a Kaalchakra show, for someone to manufacture an oil that promotes hair growth, for someone to write a book on success, promote it and make it a hit. In our times, various kinds of

Gurmeet Ram Rahims are available in different kinds of packages. Don't take it to heart. This is India. These babas are us—the same as you and I.

How We Love

1.

A Space for Love

Not everyone is in love. Nor does everyone have the courage to love. In our country, most people only love in their imagination. I wouldn't know how it is in other places, but in India, to love is to battle with innumerable strictures imposed by society and religion. Love is a forbidden subject even within the four walls of our homes. How many parents say to their children, 'Is there someone special in your life?' How many ask their daughters, 'Do you like someone? Are you in love?' With such little support, love is not a simple matter of saying 'I love you.'

We all learn to imagine love through cinema. Films are the sculptors of our divine madness. Generations of filmmakers, songwriters and musicians have burnt up their imaginations teaching us how to love. They have taught us the art of gazing at someone for the first time, and the trick of colliding with them by accident. In the process, films have turned us into lovers sometimes, and sometimes into lafangas.

Ek Duje Ke Liye (1981) was a powerful film. For the first time in Hindi cinema, lovers surmounted the barrier of language and linguistic culture and gave up their lives for the idea of a great India that is otherwise a sham shouted about from the rooftops day and night. Rati Agnihotri and Kamal Hasan, that unforgettable couple, can still make you cry. Perhaps for the first time, a popular film challenged the facile and counterfeit notion of a composite India that we have internalized for too long. 'Mere jeevan saathi/Pyar kiye ja…': to write a song by stringing together the titles of Hindi films was not mere talent; it was a way of saying that it is possible for a Hindi-wali to fall in love with a Tamil-wala. He can construct a language of love with Hindi film names. She can call out to him using the names of Tamil Nadu's districts and cities. She can talk to him and she can sing along with him.

But films have not always made us good lovers. The films coming from Mumbai kept trying only to breach the high wall between the rich and the poor—that was the extent of their revolution. 'Chandi ki deewar na todi, pyaar bhara dil tod diya/ Ek dhanwaan ki beti ne nirdhan ka daaman chhorh diya—She did not break down the walls of silver, she broke a heart full of love/A rich man's daughter betrayed a poor man in love.' (*Vishwas*, 1969) The pain of love! Rich women are always heartbreakers, always disloyal. In some films, rich women did leave everything behind to be with the love of their life, but the dominant narrative remained that in the world of love, wealth, too, is caste. Everyone should stay within the confines of their caste and explore the possibilities of love there.

Innumerable lovers have lit up the Hindi silver screen. But they are just two beautiful bodies. They have no caste, no religion. In the fantasy world of our filmmakers, love is also a fantasy. Lyricists have never written a song where a young man confronts his lover's social background. All heroes are upper caste, either Kapoor or Mathur or Saxena. Heroines have been either Lily, Mili or plain silly. The heroine drops fully formed and chaste from the skies. 'Kisi shaayar ki ghazal, Dream Girl/Kisi jheel ka kamal, Dream Girl—A poet's ghazal, Dream Girl/A lotus in a lake, Dream Girl' (*Dream Girl*, 1977).

Countless stories of Hindi cinema have put love at the service of the status quo, whereas in love you simply cannot be status-quoist. You have to first vault over the wall of caste. Films which preach Hindu-Muslim unity have very deliberately steered clear of Hindu-Muslim love stories. I cannot recall a film where a Hindu girl held the hand of a Muslim boy and said, 'I love you.' No hero has ever abandoned his Kapoor family for a Dalit girl. Oh, I'm now hoping for social change through films! Come on, Ravish.

Actually, our politics too cannot imagine a love that smashes the barriers of caste and religion. There are some Muslim leaders whose wives are Hindu. There are some Hindu leaders who are married to Muslim women. These were love marriages, but such couples do not display their love in public. They fear their voters' displeasure. But is society really like that? Yes, it is, but it is in exactly such a society that possibilities emerge for revolutionary love. People bring down the walls of caste and religion. Sometimes they do so and stay alive.

You must have noticed how often I have used the word 'wall'. That, really, is the tragedy. In India, there is no love without a wall. Love may be possible without a mehboob, the lover-beloved, but it is not possible without a wall! It's a complicated business, love. It turns you into a rebel, it makes you crazy—a baawla, a baawli. There's such tension that, as in Hindi cinema, you want to escape into a dream sequence: your trousers and shoes are suddenly white and shining. Your lover, in a flowing white gown, comes running towards you in slow motion.

You wrap yourselves around each other, and then the song begins. 'Maey se meena se na saaqi se…na paimaane se/ Dil behelta hai mera aapke aa jaane se—Not with wine, the wine-bearer or the cup/My heart is happy only with your presence.' We learnt from this song from *Khudgarz* (1987) that one's lover can also be a replacement for entertainment. There's no good song playing on TV. You've fought with your father. Forget all that and sing a song. Let's get it written by Gulzar or Anand Bakshi. Escape is the only space for love in India.

Our cities have no space for love. For us, parks are places where marigolds and bougainvillea bloom. Where a few elderly, retired people come to jog. There may be a pair or two of lovers; they will be stared at. Love needs a suitable space, just for love. Lovers in our cities get tired standing behind pillars in super-malls for hours on end. They court danger daring to love inside a car with the windows and windshield curtained with bedsheets and towels. They hold hands in the dark in a cinema and hastily let go when the lights come on. Lovers have never really told anyone of their plight. They haven't even written about it on Facebook. 'Milo na tum toh hum ghabraayen, milo toh aankh churaayen, humein kya ho gaya hai—When we don't meet my heart is restless, when we do I'm too shy to look into your eyes—oh, what's happened to me?' When you hear this song from *Heer Ranjha* (1970), don't you feel like asking—First tell us, just *where* can we meet?

But hats off to all the lovers of India. There's no place to meet, yet you don't give up, you find a way. You pull down the plastic curtains in auto-rickshaws, you squander your entire pocket money on auto fares. In search of empty cinema halls, you raise the box-office collections of trashy films. Despite the glares from passers-by, you let your head rest on your lover's shoulder. The long hours you struggle for a few moments with your mehboob transform you from lovers to activists. Everyone who has loved has known such hazards. If I were a neta, I would have built a love park in every city and would have happily lost the next election. Naturally, society would not have approved.

Snap out of this 'Ishq koi rog nahi' slumber. Of course it's a malady, this kind of love. Demand the space for love. Sixty per cent of India, all of you young people under 35, you are not here to just make nuts and bolts for machines or open shops or sell pakodas. Your youth will one day demand to know: How much time have you given to love, and how much have you spent on work? If you have only loved work, then of what use is life? If you were never possessed by the madness to look for hours into another's eyes, then what really have you seen? You might measure the dowry you get as much as you want, but you will not find a mehboob in there. Society does not want to lose control over the dowry economy, and that is why it does not easily yield space to love marriages. A woman must be the only commodity whose price is fixed by a man's worth. Money along with a bride. After all, the bride is the dowry herself. Go drown yourselves, young men of this nation. Doob maro!

Love makes us human. *That* is ishq. It makes us responsible and slightly better human beings than we were before. All lovers are not ideal humans, nor always good, but the one who is in love can at least imagine a better world. When you are in love, you discover the many nooks and corners and secrets of your city. In some places, you hold hands as you walk. In others, you walk alongside but a little far apart. Lovers want to transform the city into the city of their imagination. The city of their memories is not the city of Ghalib's poetry. True lovers know the city, they live it, too. The rhythm of the seasons beats in their hearts. Those who are not in love, they do not inhabit their city.

'Jis tan ko chhooa tune, us tan ko chhupaoon/Jis man ko lage naina, woh kisko dikhaoon—The body that you've touched, I hide that body/The heart that you've seen, I don't show it to anyone?' (*Rudaali*, 1993). Ah! We cannot even express this feeling of love here. Meera, you who sang and danced in love, you lived in this country, did you not?

Love makes us a little vulnerable, a little hesitant. And if a human being is neither, he can turn into a monster. To love is not just to say 'I love you.' To love is to know someone and, for that someone, to know yourself. It is the month of February, don't waste all your energies searching for a lover. Look for yourself, too, and for your city, a city where love is possible. And look for the dreams you want to realize for someone else's sake.

Not just eco-friendly, we must make our cities ishq-friendly as well. We must make a space where we can spend a few restful moments. Where cops don't appear, banging their lathis, when they see love. Where the defenders of honour and faith and bloodlines don't appear with guns and knives. Where the moongphaliwala doesn't appear the minute you start a conversation. It's fine that there is a space for love in our dreams. And in our films. But how is it right that our cities don't have any? It isn't right.

2.

A Death in Delhi*

A boy has died, killed on a busy road by the family of the girl he loved. In a society that lurks in the bushes to catch lovers kissing, Ankit Saxena's death is certainly not the last.

I silently look at photographs of him in happier times. He was just twenty-three. A life that had had so many hues to it has been extinguished. What must be the depth of despondency in a country where those who love are cut down by swords and knives?

Those who are waiting for someone to write on the incident in this time of all-pervading despair are already consumed with bloodlust. They are determined to clock every writing effort of a certain kind of person whom they watch closely, alarm in their hands—*now* what will he do, will he write now, about this? In a society of vultures, the act of writing increasingly feels like answering a roll-call.

How one wishes one could have seen Ankit's love blossom. Even before he died, the lovers knew they

---

*This essay is adapted from a blog I wrote on 5 February 2018, four days after twenty-three-year-old Ankit Saxena was killed in west Delhi's Raghubir Nagar.

were exchanging vows of love in the shadow of death. Why, Ankit's beloved had made up her mind to run away forever, even locked up her own parents in their house—is it not possible to love without rebelling in India? Even today young women find themselves having to flee their homes to be true to their love. They are chased down by parents brandishing sharpened swords of caste and religion.

What must be going through the mind of Ankit's beloved, whose desire to be with him made her leave home with a resolve never to return? There she was running towards the metro rail station, which resonates with the sound of modern India's approaching footsteps. On the other end were heartrending images of Ankit's mother screaming out her grief in her home in Raghubir Nagar. On both ends it is daughters who are suffering. The son, both lover and beloved, has been put to death.

Ankit was also rushing in the direction of the metro rail station where she was waiting for him. How one wishes he had reached the appointed spot that day. They would have boarded a bus together and disappeared from a world soaked in hatred, sloughing off every marker of their existing identities. But his wretched car, it had to go and collide with her mother's scooty, of all things. The newspaper reports said her mother collided with him on purpose—Ankit was surrounded. He was fatally stabbed in the neck.

Ankit Saxena was Hindu. His love is Muslim. And to make things very clear, her mother is Muslim, her brother is Muslim, her father is Muslim, her uncle is Muslim. I have no qualms mentioning someone's religious affiliation. Even if I were to refrain from mentioning this fact, it would make no difference to a society of trolls addicted to fomenting hatred—it will see what it chooses to see, namely a Hindu and a Muslim, of whom the Hindu was killed.

What would have happened had the story been inverted—if she had been Hindu, he had been Muslim and parents on both sides had been willing? Those very groups that are now trying to make political capital out of Ankit's death would have been creating a disturbance outside their doors, no question. The way the trolls are going on at the moment, it is as if they would have led the wedding procession of the star-crossed lovers. We need to ask ourselves, always—who exactly are the people spreading venom against such inter-faith marriages?

This brings to mind the immense courage shown by the father of a girl in Ghaziabad in December 2016, when those who were complete strangers to the Hindu girl and the Muslim boy came determined to cause a commotion on the day of their marriage. Undeterred, the girl's father made sure the marriage went off without any hitch, and in that very city. What happened was that the district head of a certain political party gathered a crowd outside the girl's house to disrupt the wedding proceedings. Not only did he not succeed, his party had to strip him of his position as well.

Who are the powerful people setting rules regarding who shall love whom? What are these rules doing to our society? Who is being pumped up with hatred and who is planning a kill? You can figure these things out for yourself. We'll let it be if you can't. It isn't simple, after all. Within you, too, there are layers of violence that you almost descend to before you stop yourself.

The prevailing atmosphere has enfeebled everybody. There are very few who are able to defy their weakness as the father of the girl in Ghaziabad did. Some, like the Muslim parents from Khayala, give up and become killers. How one wishes that the parents of Ankit's beloved had not treated their daughter, the brother had not treated his sister, as their commodity. Not theirs, not of any religion. Hatred has raised so many walls around us, laid so many layers of violence inside us that it is a constant struggle to overcome them. We can win the battle—or lose and become killers.

Think about the couple from Coimbatore, Kausalya and Sankar. Both were Hindus, after all. Then why was Sankar hacked with the sharp edge of a weapon in broad daylight? Why did Kausalya's parents hatch a conspiracy to kill her love? He was a Dalit and she was from an 'upper caste'. They fell in love, got married. It was when they were returning home from the market that *goondas* hired by Kausalya's parents put an end to Sankar's life. This happened in 2016. The video of the incident is terrifying.

From day one, Kausalya maintained that her parents were responsible for Sankar's murder. The investigation took a year and the case resulted in a conviction. This must be one of the few cases of honour killing to be wrapped up so soon. It would be instructive to read the details of the case, available online, for there is a great deal to learn from it. May god give Ankit's beloved the courage to do what Kausalya did. She has certainly given a statement that her parents killed Ankit.

Add the tag of 'Hindu' or 'Muslim' to every name as many times as you want, but it will not suffice to explain away the reality of the violence entrenched in our society. Just the other day, those wanting to reap the bitter harvest of communalism were collecting donations for Shambhulal Regar, the man who hacked and burnt

Mohammad Afrazul in Rajasthan and got his nephew to record the murder on his phone. These are people who want a constant supply of firewood to keep society perpetually flared up.

Honour killing is a cocktail made of prejudice, hate and misogyny to which the colour red is contributed by religion, caste, father or brother as the occasion may demand. It is not just the act of falling in love that invites honour killing. When daughters are foetuses in their mothers' wombs, they are killed in the name of family and honour. This is the truth of a community, a religion—are we prepared to accept which one? It is the truth of a country and its society. In such a country, what can the rousing slogan 'Beti bachao, beti padhao' mean? Save the daughter, educate the daughter. From whom exactly should we protect our daughters? Our daughters have so many killers facing them—first and foremost, their own mothers and fathers.

Religion and caste have always condemned us to a lifetime of fear. In a customary moment of love we may sing a note or two about taking wing like birds, but the truth is we continue to be trapped in the cage of religion and caste. The way things are in India, couples invariably find little love and far more hatred in the course of their love. That they still dare to love is worthy of our salutations.

In a society with an entire arsenal of arguments against love, there will be no real grief over the killing of Ankit; it is already looking for some benefit in the tragedy. How great, then, the words that Ankit's father has spoken—he does not want any tension in the neighbourhood. He wants justice for his son, but he won't make it about religion.

However, tension will remain. Things will not be allowed to quieten down. Anti-Romeo 'squads' set up against 'love jihad' will roam the streets, holding our daughters captive. Every killing whets the appetite for more killings. Those who are killers themselves will keep trolling you to ask when you will write about 'Hindu killings' to prove that you aren't a 'Muslim lover'.

I was trolled after Ankit's death. I was watched: Would I? Did I care? But it is they who do not care, for anyone's life or love.

This is what I have to say to them: 'Look within yourself and think about what you are doing. Aren't you among those who get couples attacked in parks and thrashed within an inch of their lives? You do not care about a boy who died. He loved. But your aim is to kill love, isn't it? You go hunting in parks to perform acts of honour killing. You should not talk of justice.

'By adding the prefix of maulana or mullah to my

name, what do you think you are doing? You are mirroring that against which you want something to be written. Your politics of hate, and the very idea of snuffing out the love that exists in every home, is proving to be fatal. The frenzy is rising. It will consume you, too. Why don't you let the country breathe a little free, give flight to its youthful dreams?'

Love can save us. But we never really let it bloom in our society. Now we've raised an army to police love and to kill it. Youngsters who do not know what it is to be in love and marry the person of their choice remain cowards forever, timid for life. Living in a society of crores of unsuccessful and timid lovers, we have become killers. First we extinguish any possibility of love that we may have—we kill our love. Then we target someone else's love.

The Fundamental Right to Privacy

Think back to what happened on 22 August 2017: there was a rush in government circles to take credit for the Supreme Court's judgement striking down the validity of instant triple talaq. In contrast, when a nine-judge Constitution bench of the Court delivered an even more historic verdict just two days later, ruling that privacy is a fundamental right, there wasn't exactly a scramble for the bouquets pouring in. The government was in a bind, and it did an awkward dance around the truth.

Since 2014, when the NDA government came to power, its attorneys general had maintained that privacy is *not* a fundamental right. However, at a press conference after the 24 August judgement, Union Law Minister Ravi Shankar Prasad tried to present the defeat handed down by the Supreme Court judgement as a victory. 'Government welcomes [the] judgement,' he said. 'Government has been of the view, particularly with regard to Aadhaar, that the right to privacy should be [a] fundamental right. The Supreme Court has affirmed what the government had said in Parliament while moving the Aadhaar Bill.'

He was referring to a statement made by Union Finance Minister Arun Jaitley in the Rajya Sabha on 16 March 2016, during the debate on the Aadhaar Bill, that 'probably, privacy is a Fundamental Right; it is too late in the day to say it is not'. Since Jaitley's somewhat equivocal statement was in tune with the ruling of the Constitution bench, why had the attorney general never made this declaration in court? Why had the government's legal counsel argued forcefully and consistently that the right to privacy cannot be a fundamental right? As the law minister was now claiming victory for the government in the Supreme Court's verdict, he should at least have told us exactly which arguments of his attorney general had been accepted by the Court and reflected in its verdict.

From the tenor of Ravi Shankar Prasad's press conference, it was clear that the enormous significance of 24 August 2017 was weighing heavily on the government. The ruling was on privacy, not Aadhaar, on which a five-judge bench would rule separately; but Prasad was holding up his Aadhaar card and reminding us of an arguably pro-privacy statement made by his fellow minister. It should have occurred to some journalist to ask this question: If what Jaitley had said during the debate on the Aadhaar Bill back in March 2016 was indeed the government's position, why was it that in a matter pertaining to Aadhaar in this very Supreme Court the then attorney general, Mukul Rohatgi, had declared that arguments which saw the indiscriminate collection of biometric data as bodily intrusion were 'bogus'—and that a citizen had no absolute right over his or her body? After that chilling submission by Rohatgi, the Government of India had an opportunity to revise its stand on privacy before the Constitution bench, but it chose not do so. Then why was Jaitley's Rajya Sabha statement being used as a smokescreen to mask the resounding defeat of the government's stand in the Supreme Court? An official statement welcoming the judgement is mere formality, a compulsion, when there is no acknowledgement of the fact that the government was in the wrong. For the people of India, it was a historic verdict, but it did not appear to be so for the Government of India.

At that hastily organized press conference a journalist did say to the law minister that he was prevaricating and misrepresenting facts, at which a look of tension spread over the minister's face. Another journalist wanted to know what the government would do about a recent bill it had introduced to prevent same-sex couples from having children through surrogacy, now that sexual choice was a fundamental right in the light of the Supreme Court ruling. Without batting an eyelid, the minister said the question was not germane to the subject of the press conference. In a manner that was far more suave, Arun Jaitley, too, attempted to put a positive spin on the matter. They were both trying to fool people, so that the government did not lose face. It is for this reason that every vigilant and reflective citizen should make it a point to read the judgment several times.

This ruling of India's apex court will be an example for the whole world. It is a judgment that will give India a new identity. Addressing the Constitution bench, the attorney general K.K. Venugopal had given the following argument: The issue of privacy concerns only the well-to-do sections of Indian society. It is completely removed from the needs and aspirations of the majority of the population. For the proper delivery of facilities that the state provides to the poor under various social welfare schemes, the right to privacy can be cast aside. The right to life is paramount, not the right to privacy. He was saying what the government and its supporters had maintained all along—that the arguments for privacy were nothing but an instance of the rich and the elite making a storm in a teacup as a pastime. But the apex court made it very clear that the government's argument did not hold water. The Court went further, observing that such a stand was a betrayal of the spirit of the

Constitution. Our Constitution puts the individual ahead of everything else. To hold that the poor are in need of economic progress alone and not civil and political rights is both wrong and dangerous.

The question is this: considering that the Government of India is elected by the people of India and represents them all, what is the intention behind this government's stand—in the Supreme Court of India, no less—that civil and political rights are fine for the well-to-do but are not pressing needs for the poor? The government is not doling out charity to the poor in the name of subsidies. It provides subsidies because it is answerable to the people, and is responsible for their welfare. In return it cannot take away other rights from them. Regardless of whether the people are starving or have full stomachs, they can form an adverse opinion of the government, mobilize against it, or come out on the streets to protest against it. The nine-judge bench of the Supreme Court has enunciated this fact so clearly that even those who stubbornly turn a deaf ear must now hear it. This is what the main judgement says: 'The refrain that the poor need no civil and political rights and are concerned only with economic well-being has been utilized though history to wreak the most egregious violations of human rights. Above all, it must be realized that it is the right to question, the right to scrutinize and the right to dissent which enables an informed citizenry to scrutinize the actions of government. Those who are governed are entitled to question those who govern about the discharge of their constitutional duties[.]'

The verdict on the right to privacy makes the citizen conscious of the entire gamut of his or her rights. These are rights that are crucial for keeping democracy alive in letter and spirit. The Supreme Court has said the right to review the government's actions, question them and disagree with them is also protected; it is what empowers citizens in a democracy, enabling them to exercise their political choice effectively. The Constitution bench cited Professor Amartya Sen's research to illustrate what can happen when a government goes unchecked—it becomes irresponsible even in circumstances of scarcity and famine. The great famine of Bengal during British rule was barely reported because of restrictions imposed on the Indian press. There was no pressure on the government to be accountable, and lakhs of people died of starvation.

This is the reason why the privacy judgement has enormous significance for each one of us. The right to privacy is the right to life itself: the right to live without fear; the right to demand justice, respect and security from governments; the right to be regarded not as subjects but as citizens. Since 2014 the prevailing political atmosphere has been such that any criticism of the government is frowned upon. If you disagree with the powers that be, you are against the leader, against the government, against the country, and against development. The Constitution bench of the Supreme Court has a clear message for the citizens: you are entirely within your rights to question and criticize the government; in fact, by making a continuous practice of it, you strengthen Indian democracy. The way I see it, not only has the Supreme Court defined privacy, it has explained to the citizen what his or her democratic obligations are and how the Constitution safeguards them.

By this ruling, the Supreme Court has not only dismissed the government's anti-people argument but also removed the contradictions and blots of its earlier judgments. It overruled two of its previous verdicts—given in the M.P. Sharma case of 1958 and the Kharak Singh case of 1961—which had said the right to privacy was not protected under the Indian Constitution. And it has done so in powerful and memorable words—Justice Chelameswar says, 'The right to privacy consists of repose, sanctuary and intimate decisions'; Justice Chandrachud writes that 'development consists of the expansion of people's freedom' and that 'to live is to live with dignity';

Justice Nariman defines privacy as 'an inalienable human right which inheres in every person by virtue of the fact that he or she is a human being'. The manner in which the nine judges have unanimously interpreted privacy stands out like an exquisite poem in a prosaic law book.

Under Article 19 of the Constitution, citizens are free to speak, assemble anywhere in a peaceful manner, move unrestrictedly and live in any place. Under Article 21, the citizen's right to life and personal liberty is protected; an individual's life can be taken only as per procedure established by law, not otherwise. The Constitution bench has now made a significant point—while the right to privacy has not been explicitly mentioned in these Articles, it would not be accurate to say they do not contain this right. For, the fragrance of the right to privacy wafts out from these rights. The right to privacy is the Constitutional basis of a person's individuality; in its absence it is not possible for him or her to live a life of dignity. An individual's desire for respect, equality and freedom are the basic pillars of the Indian Constitution. Life and freedom have not been bestowed on us by the Constitution, they have always existed; the Constitution only protects them.

The Supreme Court may not have made an inventory of all that constitutes privacy, but it has clearly stated that whom you are intimate with, whom you have a sexual relationship with, whom you marry and have children with, what kind of home and family you make for yourself are all matters that come under the rubric of privacy. The right to privacy recognizes that it is important for an individual to have control over the essential aspects of his or her life. In doing so, it also protects our cultural diversity and plurality.

The privacy judgement is not about the political regime alone. The corporate sector, too, is increasingly intruding into our lives in almost infinite ways, and often in collusion with governments. Giving this aspect considerable thought, the Constitution bench has extensively cited the prophetic novel *1984* by George Orwell, an author acclaimed for his unparalleled understanding of authoritarianism and power-crazed despots. The reference to this work is a slap in the face for all those who either opposed the right to privacy or ridiculed the demand for it. As the Constitution bench states, while *1984* was set in a fictitious state, it could very well be portraying our present reality. The manner in which technology has developed provides the potential for not only states but also big corporations and private institutions to assume the role of 'Big Brother'. At one place the bench makes the point that to mine data on the life of an individual is to acquire the power to control his or her life. The possibility of the data collected being used to throttle the voices of dissent is far greater today. Where this data shall be kept, what the terms and conditions governing it should be, and fixing accountability for its use are issues that require the enactment of strict regulations.

People of alternative sexualities are engaged in a hard struggle for their rights. The ruling on privacy will give them the strength to continue their fight. Every other day a handful of goons go on a rampage because a girl of one faith chooses to marry a boy of another faith. One hopes that this nonsense will finally come to an end—the country's highest court has given love the means to defend itself against the bigotry and violence of governments, panchayats and the police. The Constitution bench has also identified the sheer diversity of people's choice of food and dress as aspects of privacy. It has, of course, clarified that no right is absolute. There will always be reasonable restrictions. But we have been assured that in the general run of things, nobody can butt into our lives because the right to privacy is our fundamental right and it protects us, at least legally, from zealots, goons, bullies, big business and, above all, the state.

As Faizan Mustafa, one of India's finest scholars of law, has observed, a fundamental right enables citizens to keep a check on the government and not vice versa. So the verdict on privacy is a victory for every Indian. It has truly made the Supreme Court the court of the last person in the line.

Too often, our institutions have betrayed us. And now, in the twenty-first century, democracy is being continuously undermined in ways that are becoming normal. A world that, it had seemed, would allow individual freedom to grow in unprecedented ways has instead made it far easier to rob every one of us of agency. Once again, it is in our remarkable Constitution that we will find the tools to reclaim our liberty and dignity. This is what the Supreme Court has shown us—if it has failed us in the past, through the judgement on privacy, it has also reassured us that the system of checks and balances put in place by the makers of our Constitution can still be robust. There is hope.

Today, Freedom from Fear Is Freedom from the Mainstream Media*

All difference and diversity have now disappeared from the vast landscape of the mainstream Indian media. No matter what language, what proprietorship, what region, it is the same draft that is read out—shouted out—to us day after day, night after night. Propaganda is news, and abuse is debate.

What was once considered unacceptable and unethical in the public domain has been made entirely acceptable and ethical. Not only is the media celebrating existing immoralities, it is also scaling new heights of impropriety and crudity. The mainstream media's vulgarity has destroyed the norms of Indian democracy. To be vulgar and immoderate is no longer wrong, whether on the street or in the studios of news channels. This is not the work of one odd channel or anchor; hundreds of them

*This is a translation of an edited version of a speech delivered at a session of The Wire Dialogues held in New Delhi on 24 February 2019.

are at it all the time, striking every day at the roots of our citizenship.

This transformation has been made possible by the complete fusion of the mainstream media and political power. The media now recognizes the political supporter as the only kind of viewer there can be. Since the consumers and supporters of this media are adherents of the ruling ideology and political party, the dividing line between viewer and party supporter has been erased. It is by ending the sheer diversity of information in news that this section of political supporters as viewers has been created. I think of them as the 'informationless' horde. It has grown quite big, this horde, and it is everywhere. For that reason, I take it seriously, refraining from making fun of its follies. When ignorance takes the place of learning, it is no laughing matter.

Periodically, this horde is tested for its singular lack of information. For instance, following the Pulwama incident, the debate was not on why the Prime Minister hadn't addressed the nation or the media (reserving the storm of words for the election campaign that would soon begin) but on why Sachin Tendulkar had not spoken out! But the fact is, Tendulkar *had* condemned the terror attack. He had also said that India should not, however, forfeit the World Cup tie with Pakistan, because he would hate to see the country concede two points to its rivals. This too was misreported. We have made the cardinal mistake of presuming that the expansion of communication media implies the expansion of information. But that is not so. The sharp erasure of the diversity of issues leads to a deprivation of information—a state of informationlessness. And that is what has happened across a proliferating mainstream media.

The 'national curriculum' project that most news channels have been running since 2014 has been crystal clear about its intent from day one: to snuff out the engaged and aware viewer within you. Only then would the process of seizing democracy without killing it be complete. It is quite another matter that blood has flowed on the streets in the process—in the end, the informationless crowd spares no one, be it Subodh Kumar Singh or Mohammed Akhlaq. That is the kind of impact the national curriculum launched by the present-day dispensation and its media and IT cell has had. It has almost entirely overwhelmed our democracy and our consciousness of being citizens, of being the people.

The mainstream media launched its national curriculum as soon as the Modi government came to power in 2014. At its core was the idea of ensuring a continual process of Hindu-Muslim divide. For that, it was necessary to create a sense of division among citizens and ensure that it kept growing. So the media has been trying to shatter the very idea of collective citizenship. Since information and questioning are the basis of citizenship and solidarity, the possibility of either has been severely curtailed. Our mainstream media does not question the government; on the contrary, it interrogates the *people* on behalf of the government! The political line that emerged from these channels in the wake of the Pulwama blast has shown that clearly.

Enemies are being manufactured from within the ranks of citizens. To that end, a sentiment of 'Hindu frustration' and 'Muslim frustration'—armed with half-baked information—has been generated within all of us. The frustration had existed earlier too, but it has been magnified several times over and 'installed' in the media. For that reason, today's mainstream media is not the people's media—it is a media for militant Hindus. To be more accurate, it speaks for those playing politics in the name of the Hindu religion; those who champion Hindutva, not Hinduism. Five years ago, who would have thought that this Hindutva army would occupy almost ninety per cent of the mainstream media space? Yet that is exactly what has happened. And many of us, citizens of perhaps the most diverse nation the modern world has known, have begun to feel both aggressive and insecure about our faith.

This is not to say that a large majority of Indian citizens did not perceive themselves as Hindus earlier. But that effortless and civilized understanding has been replaced by a new perception of being a Hindu—one who is shorn of courage and running scared of the people standing alongside him. One who looks at the person next to him with suspicion, seeing in him a Hindu who is anti-Hindu. And, by extension, anti-national. It is for the first time that I'm seeing a Hindu who is fearful of other Hindus. Put it down as the gift of the present-day mainstream media. Its conduct goes completely against those Hindu conventions which are claimed to be superior and are constantly lauded. The *Gita* may say that anger destroys our powers of discrimination, but our news anchor who takes its name continues to rave and rant in the same breath, speaking only in anger.

The mainstream news media and social media have forged a new kind of *bhakt*. Or maybe this new kind of bhakt has helped the media become what it is today. I feel that every citizen ought to be a Kabir or Ravidas—that is, be able to challenge the practices of institutionalized religion and the political establishment of the day. Without the example of Guru Ravidas, we would not have been able to understand what purity of the mind and the heart can be. A dip in the Ganga would have been the only way to prove one's faith, and Tendulkar would have had to go to some news channel to prove his patriotism. Today's mainstream media is against all Indian traditions. What it seeks to do, and has done, is fashion a bhakt who is completely bereft of information. And he who is informationless is loveless as well. He makes a perfect foot soldier.

This is the baseline of our democratic system now. Its very basis has changed; so too its reference point. If you ask a question, you will be branded a Congress agent, a Naxal, an urban Naxal, a Hindu-hater, a Muslim-lover, and, finally, anti-Modi, which is where all accusations come to rest. It is the ultimate anti-national act. This final point of offensive defence—why do you oppose Modi who is India?—is the point where the end of our democratic system begins.

To forge a feeling of 'Hindu frustration', the media played up a fear of Muslims—in fact, the entire project of building Hindu anger has been centred on this idea. It is worth noting that the project ended up having the same impact on Muslims as it did on Hindus. Just as the Hindus stopped asking questions of the government, the Muslims, out of fear, did the same. In fact, the latter have not just stopped asking questions, they have been abandoning their political right of representation as well.

In a bid to stem further polarization in society, they are withdrawing from public and political spaces. Political parties other than the BJP have also been affected by this build-up of fear—they too have withdrawn from asking questions on these issues for fear of losing votes. Even as it is in danger of becoming entirely irrelevant, our primary opposition party cannot find the courage to return to its original ideals. It is afraid of being seen as 'anti-Hindu'.

I see before me a craven India where everybody is putting their respective fears forward. It is imperative that we regain our consciousness of being citizens, or else we stand to lose the India we attained after a century of struggle. Both Hindus and Muslims need to liberate themselves from fear. For that, they will have to free themselves of the mainstream media.

If one studies the speeches of politicians, the angry demeanour of news anchors, the slogans gracing TV screens and the language of WhatsApp messages, a certain mental complex becomes apparent. A Tendulkar whose language does not reflect that complex can be an anti-national; so too a decorated military hero like lieutenant-general Syed Ata Hasnain. Today's mainstream media has shown that stupidity, vulgarity and immoderation can provide a revenue model for good business.

It is not that this process is not being challenged. Members of the public are posing questions to the government through YouTube. A new kind of media is emerging, such as *The Wire*, *Scroll*, *The Caravan*. And there are newspapers like *The Telegraph*. We too have been making an effort at our channel. The number of those who understand what the media ought to be is gradually rising. Intrepid female journalists who are fighting the system also provide hope. In terms of the scale of what we are up against, all these efforts are small. But I have faith that these signs of hope will grow with time.

Until then, what we have is a media that is no longer the fourth estate of democracy. It is the first estate of a political party. Thanks are due to the BJP and Modi *ji* for bestowing such a spineless mainstream media on the country. Really, Modi ji, I'm tempted to ask you, like your favoured Bollywood star: where exactly do you get the temperament of a fakir? Only someone without a care for the world can give his blessings to a media such as this.

I often wonder what the Prime Minister feels when he sees himself on news channels that broadcast their pure devotion to him 24/7. Is he happy? Is he surprised? Does he spare a thought for our democracy? But then he is a fakir. Why should a fakir bother himself with all this?

Reading *1984* in 2019

If you look back at the history of the Nazi era, you will come across the word 'cleansing'. It was used in the context of the elimination of the Jews—from purging neighbourhoods of their presence by means of forced removal, to the extermination of the Jewish race itself. To systematically target and eliminate a section of the population in this manner is referred to as cleansing.

While familiarizing yourself with the contexts in which the word 'cleansing' was used by the Nazi regime, and how the project of cleansing was pursued, you might want to turn a leaf, any leaf, of George Orwell's novel *1984* as well. There is mention in it of an entity called the Thought Police. Orwell imagines an institution that reads every single thought taking shape in the minds of citizens, thus keeping them under strict surveillance. No citizen can think against the Party, write against it or speak against it. Here, there, everywhere microphones are installed; also giant telescreens. Behind the screens is someone who is watching you. And someone is listening in on you as well. The Thought Police does not want any kind of human emotion to remain alive in the citizens—

not even a feeling of unrestrained happiness. The Party controls the emotions of all citizens too.

Orwell's *1984* was published in 1949. These days the novel is being read anew in the US. How did this man manage to see our times so clearly that he could describe them precisely in cold print seventy years ago? Consider the formation of a group called Clean the Nation (CTN) in the year 2019, in India. What happens is this: A day after the Pulwama attack, i.e., 15 February 2019, nine youths form CTN on Facebook. Over the next two days, they identify people who raise questions about the Pulwama attack and then register complaints against them with the police. Those identified are trolled. Then the police arrest them (charging them with 'sedition', among other things), following which they are suspended from their universities and jobs. By this time CTN boasts 4,500 members. The page has forty administrators, most of them in their twenties, working as IT professionals in Noida and Delhi. They are united in their mission to 'clean and weed out anti-nationals'. CTN's page is banned by Facebook and Twitter cancels its handle. But CTN, which seems to be more of a front organization, soon reappears on both platforms and continues to be on the hunt.

The CTN project had started with the release of

a video featuring CTN core member Madhur Singh, wearing a T-shirt with 'Indian Army' written across it, asking people to 'Find out who is laughing at our soldiers today…Contact their employers, get in touch with the universities where they are studying…Screw them up this way. Get them dismissed from their jobs, have them suspended from their universities.'

Karishma Mehrotra of *The Indian Express* spoke to Madhur Singh and other core members of CTN. They told her their team collected information about 'anti-Indians' through Facebook because it has the most personal location details. And they claimed that a range of actions had been taken against anti-nationals in about forty-five instances: a college in Guwahati suspended an assistant professor; Rajasthan University suspended four female Kashmiri students; a twitter post led to an arrest in Jaipur; in Greater Noida an engineering college suspended a Kashmiri student; in Katihar, Bihar, a student was arrested on account of a Facebook post. Several institutions even sent CTN the letters of suspension they had issued.

Then, on 29 June 2019, an award was bestowed on CTN for social media journalism: The Social Media Patrakarita Narad Samman, instituted by an organization that goes by the grandiose name of Indraprastha Vishwa Samvad Kendra (IVSK), or Indraprashtha World Dialogue

Centre. On the dais were Manmohan Vaidya of the RSS, and union minister Smriti Irani.

The Indian Express spoke to the secretary of IVSK, Vagish Issar, who had this to say: 'This group was the recipient of the award for the simple reason that we saw how much they love their nation. Many people do so but some love their nation proactively.'

The assistant professor who was suspended from the college in Guwahati told *The Indian Express* that she had to flee from her home to escape the media's relentless pursuit of her. She returned a month later only to discover that no decision had yet been taken on her suspension. In Jaipur, a case was filed in court against the four Kashmiri girls—their WhatsApp message was read as an expression of joy over the Pulwama attack. They were suspended from their college and hostel. Some local people also demonstrated against them. An FIR was lodged against them, but mercifully there were no arrests. The SHO of the concerned police station revealed to *The Indian Express* that there was no case to be made out against the girls.

Most certainly these incidents would have fuelled a debate at a local level, in neighbourhoods, offices and housing colonies. Fake information must have been used to stoke jingoistic feelings among people. The media too would have jumped right into the high-decibel debate.

Now the matter has been put to rest, but neither society nor the media has suffered any pangs of regret. Everywhere, issues are manufactured for contentious debates in this manner. 'Anti-nationals' are spotted every other day and denounced and persecuted. Every day a new case is made so that people stray from the real issues that should concern them; issues for which the government would otherwise have to answer. This is the daily drill now. People have become citizens of *1984*—they exist in an Orwellian universe. They no longer have a mind of their own, no sense of discernment. So much so that they can't even laugh when they want to—they can only laugh when and as much as the leader and his government ask them to.

The CTN gang is not the only 'police' around, there are many others. Even if they aren't at your doorstep yet, there is the constant fear of their impending arrival. You feel apprehensive about writing freely and publicly. You hold yourself back from speaking uninhibitedly for fear of a troll attack. Groups like CTN are watching you. Big Brother is watching you. Groups like CTN are Big Brother's CCTV camera.

Welcome to the new Republic. You are no longer a citizen; you have become the Party. Those who have not, and must pay the price, are not your concern.

I'm reminded again of the word 'cleansing', with which I began. The Nazis' project of cleansing started with the Jews. Then other sections of the population were added to the list. It became a long list, it kept growing. In her essay 'The Other Victims of the Nazis', the writer Ina R. Friedman reminds us that in addition to six million Jews, the Nazi regime killed over five million others who were considered racially impure, anti-German, unhealthy, unproductive or immoral. Among them were gypsies, blacks, Jehovah's Witnesses, the physically and mentally disabled, Communists, Social Democrats and other political opponents of the Nazis, dissenting clergy, homosexuals, transgenders, prisoners of war, epileptics, alcoholics, Slavic peoples, painters, writers, musicians and other artists whose opinions and works Hitler disliked...

Friedman writes, '[The legislation] subtitled "The Law to Remove Stress from the People and State"...allowed the Nazis to completely ignore the civil and human rights previously guaranteed by the German constitution. In addition to passing laws legalizing their denial of human rights, the Nazis began a press and radio propaganda campaign to portray their intended victims as rats, vermin, and *Untermenschen* (subhumans).'

Then she makes an observation which brings history to our own doorstep. Belief in a pure 'master race' was not unique to Hitler and the Nazis, she points out. What was unique was how enthusiastically different sections of German society, including scientists, doctors, anthropologists, engineers and students, cooperated in the process of identifying and eliminating 'undesirable groups'. They were cleaning the Fatherland by weeding out anti-nationals.

As you read Orwell's *1984*, don't forget to take a look at Friedman's essay as well. It is available online.*

---

*https://www.socialstudies.org/sites/default/files/publications/se/5906/590606.html

Let's Treat Ourselves to an Ice Cream This Independence Day

As the calendar ticks over to 15 August, many people start questioning the achievements made by the country since Independence. They feel some sort of 'August Fifteenth' hollowness that we have achieved nothing. The question of what we achieved or didn't, and the journey of achievement itself, is infinite.

India has come a long way in just over seventy years of Independence. Whichever corner of the world we may be in, we can take pride in this nation. It was we, the people, who made this country worth taking pride in and we will keep doing that. There will always be some room for betterment but it is the effort towards that betterment which makes the people of India, Indians. Instead of asking what has been achieved, we must start asking what we can achieve. And instead of big actions we must start with the small.

But we will not find the answer we seek only in the desire do something. We will find it also in the path we choose for ourselves. Do we manage to work at analyzing those financial and political systems which have forever claimed to be of benefit to everyone? Do we recognize the signs of democracy being robbed of the democratic spirit? Do we demand that financial growth should be about economic security for every citizen and not about a stock market boom?

Financial inequality is something that even those countries which are considered to be the Lords of Development have not managed to eradicate. The stresses of our lives haven't lessened even after we've collected the various technological conveniences of the age. Therefore we have almost all agreed to choose the easy way out: that of not trying to find a new system and, on the other hand, supporting a system which benefits only a few people. And once we have made that choice, we join that group of the chosen few or continually polish our abilities so that we can enter those hallowed halls.

Many a time, we also conflate spiritualism with financial achievement when the truth is that the two have different trajectories. We cannot be a part of economic progress without being consumerist and we cannot be spiritual while remaining consumerist. We can, of course, achieve a balance between the two.

The war for Indian Independence is a wonderful document in world history. For more than ninety years, we kept fighting to bring to life our dream of Independence. It was a war in which people of many communities and religions—even though they were fighting amongst themselves—were engaged for the nation. We were all beginning to understand that there would be no place for class differences in free India. We were stressing on the principle that there would be no place for religious hatred either. We had accepted the principles of tolerance and love as vital.

We also kept arguing about the ways in which we were to achieve Independence, and kept striving that everyone should find a life of equality and dignity in free India. When India was achieving its geographical and political existence in the context of the nationalisms of the twentieth century, it left no issue untouched, no question unasked.

However, the plague of communal riots which has always afflicted India did not stop even during the fight for freedom, when most people had banded together for the sake of the country. Riots are the legacy of British rule. If you analyze the various episodes of the politics of the loudspeaker—the eternal, easily trotted out controversy of the volumes at which maulvis in mosques can call out the azaan—and religious processions—when Hindus march into Muslim neigbourhoods with the intention to provoke, and vice versa—you will find a terrifying continuity in modern Indian history, from before Independence to after. It was perhaps as a retaliation to this madness that Bhagat Singh declared himself an atheist and the editor and reporter Ganesh Shankar Vidyarthi was martyred while trying to stem a communal riot in Kanpur. Today, the number of people who spread hatred by highlighting this reason or that or by exploiting various inequalities has increased exponentially. They want all reckonings to be made immediately. Any one incident is ascribed to an entire community—this is done by both sides—and the politics of hatred begins.

In 2014, a story emerged from Sarawa village in the Meerut district of Uttar Pradesh. A twenty-year-old woman who taught Hindi in a local madrasa alleged that she had been kidnapped by the village head, forcibly converted to Islam and gangraped. It sparked a great deal of aggressive mobilization on social media and all of Meerut remained tense for a while. And while the case was still being investigated by the local police, it was also used as an excuse to try to justify those episodes in which someone from the Muslim community had been killed or sexually violated.

It is only he who seeks to spread hatred who can take a criminal act and make it part of a 'war' for religious 'pride'.

With time, the episode in Meerut became controversial after questions were raised about the woman's claims during police investigations. And, as soon as questions were raised, the hate squads decamped.

When the controversy about the incident was raging, I received numerous phone calls demanding to know why I didn't raise and talk about such issues. And I remember wondering why most of the calls that came to me were from people who sought to find religious overtones in everything and spread madness. Why didn't a single person tell me that no, these are fabricated issues which must be ignored or we risk spreading poison in society? Why didn't these people ever call in with requests to discuss life-affirming, life-affecting questions? And another thing, many of the callers delivered threats, warning me of what might befall if I didn't raise the issue. Yet, ironically, these very same people declared that they were generous and broad-minded as far as religion was concerned. How can he who is generous and broad-minded ever talk about hatred and deliver threats of violence?

This is something we must all collectively decide. Do we want to spread hatred on the basis of sundry reasons, whether real or imagined, or to eradicate it? He who believes in hatred does not need reasons at all. He will always find some community or the other to hate. What is important is that we push these people to the margins.

Can hatred be justified by any argument, ever? There are any number of stories of legal justice not being delivered in this country; should they be used as an excuse to pour poison into society? Did the media cover a certain person or issue or not is certainly a question that should be asked. But should it be asked in such a manner that its only objective is to spread hate?

If we do not have compassion within ourselves, we will never understand what it means to be Hindu, or Buddhist, or Muslim. No one can be religious without compassion. A person without compassion is a savage underneath the veneer of piety and religiosity. For him, religion becomes a means to establish domination. Religion ultimately teaches you to be tolerant.

Some people—perhaps those who feel that August Fifteenth hollowness within themselves—ask me why they should celebrate Independence Day. After all, according to them, nothing has been achieved.

I tell them that if you have achieved dominance

over any kind of hatred within yourself, increased your levels of tolerance, you have full right to celebrate the Independence of India. If you don't hate another religion or community, you can celebrate Fifteenth of August. If you have raised your voice against hatred, or faced a conflict, a war, within yourself, you can celebrate Fifteenth of August. If you understand that Bhagat Singh was martyred for you, Khudiram Bose stepped on to the gallows for your sake, and Mahatma Gandhi took bullets in his chest for you, you should indeed celebrate the Fifteenth of August.

What isn't acceptable, I tell them, is for you to hate a certain community and still wear the martyrdom of Bhagat Singh like a crown upon your head and declare that you are a patriot. If you haven't done this, you have kept alive those dreams of India which lakhs of people sacrificed their lives to achieve. Independence Day is yours.

There is much to do still, many areas which we must work on. But if we remain aware of those areas, of the work that needs doing, we can rest for one day and celebrate Independence Day. We may eat an ice cream, a gulab jamun, two jalebis. We could also buy some sweets and distribute them among those less fortunate than ourselves. That which is good and right within us has come to be because of the dream of that India which the numerous generations that have come before us have woven together like a beautiful sweater. The sweater whose soft warmth makes our hearts large and generous. Which gives us courage to celebrate the momentous event that Independence is.

The Power of Citizens' Journalism to Advance Democracy

[Publisher's Note: This is the full text of the speech Ravish Kumar delivered in Manila at the presentation ceremony of the Ramon Magsaysay Awards for 2019. He was honoured with the award for 'harnessing journalism to give voice to the voiceless' and for his 'unfaltering commitment to a professional, ethical journalism of the highest standards'.]

Namaskaar.

India has conquered the moon. In this very proud moment, I am looking at the moon and at the ground beneath my feet simultaneously. My streets have craters and potholes which outnumber those on the moon. Across the world, democracies on fire in broad daylight are craving the coolness of the moon. But this fire can only be doused with information that is pure and with courage, not by mere rhetoric. The more pure our information, the deeper the trust among our citizens. Information helps build nations. Fake news, propaganda and false history, on the other hand, create mobs.

I'm thankful to the Ramon Magsaysay Foundation for giving me this opportunity to present my views to other parts of the world. As you know, I am a pure Hindiwala; for your benefit my friends have translated this lecture in English, so pardon my pronunciation and some misplaced articles.

Two months ago, I was working on my daily broadcast in my corner office when I received a call on my cell phone. The caller ID flashed an unknown international number from the Philippines. I was certain it was a troll calling. For some reason, a lot of my troll calling traffic comes from the Philippines. If they are all indeed living in the Philippines then I would like to take this opportunity to welcome them: I am here now! Anyway, coming back to that day, I turned to my colleague and asked her if she'd be interested in listening to the language used by my trolls. I put my phone on loudspeaker and from the other end was greeted by a female voice which asked, 'May I please speak to Mr Ravish Kumar?' I have received thousands of calls from trolls in my life but never from a woman. I quickly shut off the speaker and put the phone against my ear. In sophisticated English, the caller informed me that I had won the Ramon Magsaysay Award.

Flash forward to this moment, when I'm here with

you. I am not here alone. I have brought with me the entire world of Hindi journalism practised by people like Ganesh Shankar Vidyarthi and Peer Munis Mohammad.

We are living in testing times, as journalists and as common citizens. Our citizenship itself is on trial right now—and make no mistake, we need to fight back. We need to rethink our duties and responsibilities as citizens. I believe that in these times, when the assault on our citizenship is all-encompassing and the state's surveillance apparatus is more overbearing than ever, the individuals or groups who are able to withstand this onslaught and emerge stronger from it will be the ones who lay the foundation for a better citizenry and, for that matter, maybe even better governments in the future.

Our world is filled with such determined citizens already; people who in spite of pervasive hatred and a manufactured information deficit, have chosen to fight back and bloom like the cactus flower does in the midst of a barren, hopeless desert. Standing alone and surrounded by the desert stretching endlessly on all sides, the cactus doesn't think about the meaning of its existence: it stands there to let you know that it is possible. Wherever the fertile plains of democracy are being subverted into deserts, the exercise of citizenship and the fight for the claim over—and the right to—information have become perilous, but not impossible.

Citizenship requires a free flow of verifiable information. The state today has established full control over media corporations. The implication of this control over the media and in turn your information flow is that it limits and narrows the scope of your citizenship. In other words, the controlled media controls the diversity of news stories, and specifies what interpretations of news events are acceptable. The media is now a part of the surveillance state. It isn't the fourth estate anymore, but the first estate.

News channel debates take place within a vocabulary of exclusionary nationalism, wherein they seek to replace the collective history and memory of the nation with the ideology of the ruling party and of their viewers. There are only two types of people in this news universe narrative: the anti-nationals and all others. It's the classic 'us' and 'them' technique. They tell us that the problem with anti-nationals is that they ask questions, disagree and dissent. Disagreement is the aatma—the soul, or essence—of democracy and citizenship. The democratic aatma is under relentless attack every day. When citizenship is under threat; when its very meaning has been altered, then what happens to the nature of a citizen's journalism?

Both are citizens: those who claim to speak as the nation, and the victims of their derision.

There are many countries in the world where such a regime, which co-opts the judiciary too, has gained legitimacy amongst people. And yet, when we see what's happening in Hong Kong and in Kashmir, we realize that people are still out there fighting for their citizenship. Do you know why the millions of people fighting for democracy in Hong Kong have renounced social media? Because they could no longer trust a language that they knew their government speaks better than them. And so they created their own language and communicated protest strategies and tactics in this newfound syntax. This is an innovative vision of the fight for citizenship.

In order to save their rights, the citizens of Hong Kong are creating parallel spaces where lakhs of people now talk in a new register. Where they fight in new, innovative ways and gather at and disperse from protest sites in a matter of minutes. Where they have created their own apps and have altered the use of electronic metro-cards. They have modified their phones' SIM cards. The citizens of Hong Kong have challenged the government's effort to render citizenship hollow by refashioning objects of control into devices of liberation. The citizens of Hong

Kong were willing and able to extricate themselves from the authoritarian network of information. This tells us that the state has not yet defeated citizenship.

Kashmir is another story. An information and communication blackout has been imposed for several weeks now. More than ten million people cut off from any information trade whatsoever. There's an internet shutdown. Mobiles rendered useless. Can you imagine a citizen without information? What happens when the media, which is meant to gather, process and relay information, supports the shutdown of all sources of information? In doing so, the media stands against the citizen who is trying to learn about the world around her—not as a matter of curiosity, but for her very survival and her family's well-being.

It is an unfortunate coincidence that most of India's neighbours are also its neighbours on the press freedom index. India, Pakistan, China, Sri Lanka, Bangladesh, Myanmar, all fall within a few ranks of each other, right at the bottom of the international press freedom index released by reporters without borders. Freedom can have various manifestations. There is the freedom of saying what one wants. Then there is the freedom of being able to refuse what one does not want to say. There is the freedom of being able to decide the course of one's speech and thought, and here I am referring specifically to the media.

Note that I am talking here about two of the most important nations in the Indian subcontinent. A few days ago, going through my Twitter feed, I encountered a notification issued by the Pakistani electronic media regulatory authority which gave clear directions to the country's news channels on reporting the situation in Kashmir. Very aptly—and un-ironically—titled 'Advice', the directions in the notification included suspending all Eid celebrations as a token of mourning; reporting news of Indian atrocities on minorities; telecasting news which was in solidarity with Kashmiris; and observing 15th August as a black day. The notification was specific to the extent of recommending the use of only black and white colours on TV channel logos on the 15th of August, which happens to be India's Independence Day.

One wonders how such directions are to be followed. The visual drama of the television screen relies heavily on its use of colours—bright reds and greens and yellows. I wonder how Pakistani news channels managed to work on the 15th with such a limited colour spectrum, since closer home, in India, I cannot imagine TV channels running their logos and graphics in less than ten colours and shapes at any given point in the day.

And one only has to look at the kind of headlines which are used on Indian TV channels with respect to Pakistan. Every night, our 8 or 9 pm news shows carry flashy, apocalyptic headlines, turn every piece of casual news into an insult for Pakistan and keep viewers hooked while they have their dinner under the blaring cacophony of the anchors and their panellists shouting themselves hoarse. Recently, the Press Council of India sent an application to our Supreme Court supporting the media ban in the Kashmir valley, citing its commitment to 'national interest' and keeping up 'high standards of public taste'. The Editor's Guild took cognisance of the matter and issued a letter condemning the Press Council, saying the Council was working against journalists.

Naturally, the Press Council backtracked and issued a statement, declaring in bold letters that it did *not* support restrictions on the media.

Such incidents are almost amusing, but have grave implications for our freedoms as viewers and citizens. Freedom here has become a farce. When those who are meant to safeguard the reporter's right to report make a mockery of freedom in obvious and brazen ways, not only is our intelligence as viewers insulted, but the very imagination of citizen journalism begins to weaken.

When mainstream journalism can neither support its own rights nor the sheer idea of journalism, citizen journalists and citizen journalism are both under constant, existential threat. The threat here is not merely to the practical implications of reportage, viewership or financial sustenance, but also to the atmosphere which should not enable the growth and nurture of such hypocrisy and bankruptcy. Such media—and may I go so far as to say that its audiences too—cannot stand for pure information and hard facts, be it anywhere in the world. The mainstream media has moved so far away from its foundational ideals and principles, that it will—indeed, it already does—fail to see the irony and tragedy in the cases that I have just listed.

This is the same media that promoted 'citizen journalism' to reduce operating costs for itself. It outsourced its risk to you!

Citizen journalism within mainstream journalism is different from citizen journalism outside mainstream journalism. In the early days of social media when people began asking hard questions online, the old-school media houses had turned against social media and critiqued it. Blogs and websites were blocked inside newsrooms. Even today, several newsrooms do not allow reporters to express their personal opinion. It is another matter, however, that when the twenty-four-year-old woman 'Riverbend' started documenting the Iraq war and its devastation in the form of everyday blogs (which were later published as the 2005 book *Baghdad Burning: Girl Blog from Iraq*), prominent media houses around the world conceded that their reporters could not have done what this unnamed girl had done through social media.

Today, if a Kashmiri girl decided to write a blog on the lines of *Baghdad Burning*, our mainstream media would label her as anti-national. The media today is increasingly delegitimizing the space of citizen journalism because it is not interested or invested in journalism. Under the garb of journalism, the media is today the comprador of the state.

In my opinion, citizen journalism is the need of the hour when the media and mainstream journalism turn hostile to information. When the struggle for information itself is described as anti-national, and disagreement is decried as treason, 'testing time' is a meek euphemism for where we are today. When the media turns against the citizen, then it is time for the citizen to take on the role of the media. She has to do so knowing that the chances of success are slim in these times of state brutality and surveillance. The state is becoming increasingly opaque and blocking information.

The mainstream media seeks profit maximization above everything else, and this singular motive compels it to serve as a PR agent of the state. Government advertising forms a huge chunk of revenue for the media today. Citizen journalism, on the other hand, is struggling to survive purely on public support whilst staying outside the web of government patronage and advertisers.

India's mainstream media is working night and day to convert our citizens into 'post-illiterates'. It has given up on trying to convert superstitious beings into rational thinking beings. Its syllabus is comprised of unthinking 'nationalism' and communalism. The mainstream media has begun to consider the state's narrative as pure information. There are numerous channels on television but the manner and content of news on all these channels is the same. Opposition is a derogatory word for this media.

India is a great nation, and it has magnificent achievements to show for it that are pre-eminent in the world. However, a majority of its mainstream and television media has gone to the dogs. Indian citizens possess a great passion for democracy, but every night news channels arrive to trample over that passion. While evening in India may arrive with the setting of the sun, it is the reportage from news media that spreads the darkness of night.

Yet democracy is actually alive and kicking among the people of India. Every day, there are vociferous demonstrations against the government, but the media has a screening process wherein it decides to keep these protests out of the bulletins. There is no reportage of these protests, since for the media they are a futile activity.

No democracy can be a democracy without public demonstrations. As a result, the people involved in these demonstrations have now begun recording videos themselves. In these videos recorded on their phones, they take on the role of journalists, providing a break-down of the scene of action, later sharing the videos on the WhatsApp groups of the participants in the demonstration.

The definition of citizenship trumpeted by the media doesn't allow for the raising of slogans against the state. This is why citizens are attempting to preserve that essential part of themselves by creating videos for their WhatsApp groups. They have begun to upload their videos on YouTube. Agitators have begun to practice citizen journalism. By uploading their videos on YouTube, agitators have become citizen journalists.

When the state and media unite to control citizens, is it possible for a citizen to be able to act as a journalist? To be a citizen and exercise the associated rights, it requires a system that has to be provided for by the same democracy that the citizen belongs to. If the judiciary, police, and media become hostile towards the citizen, and the part of society that is aligned with—is indistinguishable from—the state begins excluding citizens, how much can we expect a defenceless citizen to fight? Yet, the citizen is fighting back. The cactus is coming alive. Every day I receive 500 to 1000 messages on WhatsApp, sometimes more. In every second message, people, alongside their problems, also write about what journalism means to them. Mainstream media may have forgotten what journalism is, but the people remember how it should be defined.

Every time I open my WhatsApp to check for updates on my office group, I never even make it that far. Instead I get caught up in the messages from thousands of people sharing their news. Trolls publicized my number in an attempt to send abuse my way. The abuse arrived, as did threats. They continue to. But so did the people, bringing with them their stories and news from their regions. Stories and news that, in the understanding of news channels, were finished and irrelevant. When they face trouble themselves, the viewers of these mainstream news channels realize what journalism means. The meaning of journalism has not yet been erased from their minds.

When the ruling party boycotted my show, all paths were closed to me. At that time, it was these people who filled my show with their issues. As the mainstream channels maintain the illusion of a functioning media among the people by outsourcing even voices against journalism and power in the name of citizen journalism, this group of citizens made me a citizen journalist within mainstream media. This is the future of the media. Its journalists need to become citizen journalists just so that people can be citizens.

While common people were being erased from news channels and a single political agenda was being shoved down their throats, some people didn't stop trying to break free of this nexus. In the midst of all the abuse and intimidation, the number of messages making demands on the government started rising. I started getting trolled by the issues of the people. 'Will you not speak up for us? Are you afraid of the government?' they asked me, incessantly.

I started listening to them. My show Prime Time's temperament changed. Thousands of young men and women began to message me, telling me how central and state administrations would not conclude examinations for government jobs even two or three years after they were declared. Job appointment letters would not be sent even after results were published. If I were to ballpark the number of youngsters involved in all these exams, then the number of men and women waiting for their results would come to around one crore, or ten million. As late as 2018, Bihar, the state that I come from, had not published results of exams conducted in 2014. The impact of Prime Time's 'job series' was soon felt and many pending exam results were published and appointment letters issued.

My WhatsApp number has become a public newsroom. When my secret sources within political parties and the government began to distance themselves from me, the public became my open resource. Prime Time has become increasingly reliant on people's WhatsApp messages. This was our subversion of the WhatsApp campaign launched by those in power against me. On the one hand, party 'IT cells' spread communal hate and xenophobia by bombarding broadcast lists and groups with millions of messages, and on the other hand real news was travelling to me through the same medium.

My newsroom has shifted from NDTV's newsroom to being among the people. There is still hope for India's democracy, because neither have people given up on their expectations of the government, nor have they stopped posing questions to the government. That is the reason why they are looking for an opening in mainstream media.

While the mainstream media parroted the falsehood

that Indian universities were rising in global rankings, students from countless colleges sent me their classroom and staff strengths. Had these students not approached me, how could I have reached out to a college with 10 or 20 teachers and 10,000 students? Journalism is never complete without citizens and citizenship; it is an exercise of the latter in the service of the former. In times when the media was defining the citizen per the state's parameters, citizens began to define me in their terms. The cactus flowers of hope began to bloom in this democracy.

I still remember the message I received from a girl in Chandigarh. She was watching Prime Time when her father turned off the television. She did not heed her father and went on watching the show. She is a citizen of India's democracy. As long as that girl is there, democracy will be able to surmount the challenges in front of it. I also want to mention here that many of the people who trolled and abused me have apologized of their own accord. If I have received lakhs of abuses, then I have received thousands of such messages too.

I also remember the boy from Maharashtra who was so distraught by the hatred being spouted during a news debate on his shop's television that he left to find solitude elsewhere. When he tried to watch Prime Time at home, his brother and father insisted he turn it off because they said I was anti-national. The mainstream media and the IT cell have run this campaign against me. And they have run it well, for the willing compliance of citizens in restricting the information available to them is a sign of legitimized surrender, of abdication.

I say this because in order to be a citizen journalist today, you have to struggle with the state and the citizen who is behaving per the state's desires. The challenge is not merely the state, but in equal and often greater measure those who have acted to supplement its will: the people who take it upon themselves to commit atrocities that they think the state is too constrained to perform. Media and social media contribute to the process of isolating, silencing, and intimidating citizens by placing them in the midst of mobs, virtual and real. The perception of risk rises—and the experience of fear paralyses. Today's citizens are under immense pressure. The challenge before them is to find out how to fight against this media which runs its business in their name.

We are at that moment in time when people will have to push against the barricade of the media if they want to reach the government. Otherwise their voice will continue to haunt WhatsApp inboxes. The people will have to first become citizens and then remind the state that its duties also entail the creation and nurturing of an atmosphere of fearlessness where citizenship can flourish. The government is also responsible for creating an atmosphere where the state can be questioned. You can evaluate a government only when the media is independent and free during its time.

After information, the next in line under attack is history, which gives us our strengths and our inspirations. That history is being snatched away from us. It was the same during the independence movement. Bal Gangadhar Tilak, Mahatma Gandhi, Dr. Ambedkar, Ganesh Shankar Vidyarthi, Pir Muhammad Yunus—the list is endless. They were all citizen journalists. In 1917, during the days of the Champaran satyagraha, Mahatma Gandhi asked the press in a letter to not come to Champaran for a few days, and to generally stay away from the area. He then started meeting farmers and listening to their stories. The people of Champaran made a newsroom around Gandhi. They started telling him about their complaints and provided proof. The history of India's independence struggle from then on is there for all to see.

No nation could or can exist without news. The nation as a community came about because the true stories of those we thought our own stoked our imagination. Every nation is different. The curiosity—and concern—

for the well-being of others, and especially the weakest among us, made our struggle for independence in India special. It is of utmost importance for any nation that information be factual. If information is not true and factual, trust between citizens will diminish. And that is why there is a dire need for citizen journalism once again: journalism that is independent of the business strategy of the mainstream media.

Even in these times of despair there are numerous people who are trying to fill this gap. From comedy routines to YouTube channels, they have tried to keep the essence of journalism alive: an exercise of citizenship in the service of citizens. It is their strength and determination which has not let everything become one-sided in India's democracy. Even if they have not won the battle yet, the people continue to fight.

In his prayer meeting on the 12th of April 1947, Mahatma Gandhi discussed newspapers. His comments can be quite useful for today's divisive media. Gandhi recounted how a leading newspaper of the time had published a report alleging that no one in the Congress Working Committee was paying any heed to him. His reaction to this report was that if the newspapers were not going to be authentic, then India's freedom was of no use.

Newspapers are scared today. Any criticism is seen as an invective against the nation. My criticism of the mainstream media, and in particular of news channels, is intended for the sole purpose of my great country. India's newspapers and news channels today incite and provoke conflict between communities. Gandhi had said: You should throw away these wretched newspapers. If you want any news, ask each other. If you do want to read, then carefully choose those newspapers which are being run in the service of India's citizens; those that teach Hindus and Muslims to stay together.

Had Gandhi been alive, he would have said what he did on the 12th of April 1947, and what I am repeating here today.

We are in urgent need of citizen journalists in these times. But even more than that, we need the citizen democrat.

I would like to thank the millions of viewers who watch NDTV. I am thinking today of all my colleagues at NDTV. I am thinking of Dr Prannoy Roy and Radhika Roy.

My journalism is in Hindi but I have received love across all languages in India—Marathi, Gujrati, Malayalam, Bangla. I belong to everyone. India turned me into a citizen.

I will always remember my history professors. I am

also thinking of my idol Anupam Mishra, who came to Manila with Chandi Prasad Bhatt. I miss Anupam ji a lot. My friend Anurag is here. My daughters and my life partner Nayana are here. I have walked in Nayana's footsteps to arrive here. I hope you too will follow in the footsteps of intelligent women. I hope you become good citizens.

Modi, Shah Have Been Lying About Gandhi. Here's What He Really Said About Minorities.

Those people from three neighbouring countries who belong to minority communities, and have fled to India to escape persecution, have been provided a measure of help and relief by the Citizenship Amendment Act, 2019; they have been shown some leniency. These concessions are not necessarily the outcome of Modi's thinking. It is not that the idea materialized in Modi's mind overnight and Modi made it happen. These concessions conform to the very spirit of Gandhi's thought. Mahatma Gandhi said so—those who have used his name to pontificate about the state of the nation and continue to use his surname for their vested interests, better listen carefully. Gandhi ji said so—you may or may not believe Modi, but at least believe Gandhi! Mahatma Gandhi has said, whenever our Hindu and Sikh brothers and sisters living in Pakistan feel they want to come to India, they are welcome. Mind you, I am not the one saying this but our venerable Mahatma Gandhi.

The above statement is part of the speech Prime Minister Narendra Modi delivered at the Ramlila Ground in Delhi on 22 December 2019. I'm writing this exactly a month after that rally. I deeply regret to inform you that our prime minister can utter lies even about Mahatma Gandhi. While it takes no more than a moment to utter a falsehood, it may take as long as a decade to catch that lie. Gandhi never said it the way it has been conveyed—that our Hindu and Sikh brethren from Pakistan can come to India whenever they want. On the contrary, Gandhi never tired of saying that if the minorities in Pakistan and India were to die fighting the injustice meted out to them by their respective governments, it would make him happier.

Union home minister Amit Shah did one better than Modi. On 16 January 2020, he went for a meeting in Vaishali district, Bihar complete with a written note which he proceeded to read out, saying it was what Gandhi had said on 26 September 1947: 'Mahatma Gandhi said that from every point of view the Hindus and Sikhs living in Pakistan were qualified to come to India. The first and foremost duty of independent India was to see that they got jobs, the amenities required for a comfortable existence, and citizenship.'

Did Mahatma Gandhi actually say it the way Modi and Shah claim he did?

I have before me a two-volume collection of Gandhi's prayer discourses in Hindi, *Prarthana Pravachan*, which has been published by the Delhi-based Raza Foundation and Rajkamal Prakashan. This collection contains all the prayer discourses given by Gandhi from 1 April 1947 to 29 January 1948. It would be instructive to read the discourse of 5 July 1947, especially this part of it:

> *But Pakistan's real test will lie in how it treats the nationalist Muslims, Christians, Sikhs and Hindus who live there. Moreover, there are many sects among Muslims themselves. Shias and Sunnis are the well-known ones, but there are many others too, and how they are treated remains to be seen. Will they fight with the Hindus or develop a friendship with them?*

Here Gandhi is clearly stating that there aren't just Shias and Sunnis in Pakistan; there are other Muslim sects as well. He wants to see how Pakistan deals with them. It was precisely this point that was raised by the opposition during the debate in the Parliament on the Citizenship (Amendment) Bill (now an Act)—namely, that by linking the issue with religion, the government was shutting the door on such groups among Muslims who may be persecuted; that the move was not in accordance with the spirit of the Constitution and Gandhi's principles.

The government's thinking would have been on predictable lines: 'Who reads Gandhi these days? The Hindi newspapers will publish only what we say. Taking it for the unvarnished truth, the reader will carry on animated discussions in the park about how Modiji is doing what he is only for the good of the country.'

That is exactly what happened. The Hindi newspapers have not published anything about how Modi and Shah have incorrectly presented Gandhi's statements. In other words, they have lied.

The first concern Gandhiji raises, in his discourse of 5 July 1947, is regarding the treatment of nationalist Muslims in the new nation of Pakistan. The question is: who is this nationalist Muslim who will be residing in Pakistan?

For an answer to this question, let us look at those sections of the discourses of 10 and 12 July 1947 where Gandhi clearly states who this nationalist Muslim of Pakistan is.

In the discourse of 10 July 1947, he says:

> *If people flee their homes in Sindh and other places out of fear and come here, shall we turn them away? If we do so, with what face shall we call ourselves Indians? How can we chant the slogan Jai Hind? Welcome them, saying, 'This too is your country, just as that is your*

> *country.' This is how we should deal with them. If nationalist Muslims are also forced to leave Pakistan and come here, then they too will live here. As Hindustanis, we all have the same standing. If this cannot be, then Hindustan cannot come into being.*

On 12 July 1947, Gandhi said:

> *Many Muslims come to meet me these days. The mention of Pakistan makes them nervous. The apprehension of Christians, Parsis and other non-Muslims is understandable, but why should Muslims be afraid? They say, 'We are considered quislings [traitors]. The problems we encounter will be far greater than the troubles the Hindus will face in Pakistan. As soon as the government is in full control, our association with the Congress will be deemed an offence under the Shariat.' If this is what Islam means, then I do not accept it. How can the nationalist Muslims be called quislings? I trust that just as Jinnah Saheb will protect non-Muslim minorities, so will he defend these Muslims.*

This part of the discourse of 12 July 1947 makes it amply clear that the nationalist Muslim is one who walks on the path set by Gandhi, and is associated with the Congress. At the same time, he is apprehensive that to continue an association with the Congress in the new nation of Pakistan would be seen as an offence under the Shariat. The background to this apprehension is to be found in the tussle between the Muslims who supported the Congress and those who backed the Muslim League. Historian Yasmin Khan has dealt with this issue extensively in her book, *The Great Partition: The Making of India and Pakistan*.

As is well known, the British government had decided to hold talks about independence only with elected representatives, hence elections to the central and provincial legislative assemblies were held from December 1945 to March 1946. In those elections, there were reserved seats for Muslims where only Muslim voters could elect Muslim candidates. There was intense competition between the 'League-i' Muslims and 'Congress–i' Muslims for those seats. In Muslim neighbourhoods, the Congress-i Muslims became increasingly isolated. They suffered the ire of League supporters, even getting roughed up, but remained steadfast on Gandhi's path. For that they were dubbed 'kafir' by the maulanas supporting the Muslim League. On his part, the head of the Jamiat ul Ulema had issued a fatwa against Jinnah in 1945, calling him 'Kafir-e-Azam'.

The object of Gandhi's concern is this nationalist Muslim who consistently rejected Jinnah—in India, and in the newly formed nation of Pakistan, too. This was a time when in addition to taking a stand against Jinnah, the nationalist Muslim found himself ranged against his very own within his home and family. After Partition many nationalist Muslims stayed on in Pakistan, but that did not mean they had placed their faith in Jinnah's Pakistan. These were the Muslims who came to Gandhi and said that they felt afraid to be in Jinnah's Pakistan.

Many Muslims rejected Jinnah's Pakistan and came to India. Otherwise, a great actor like Dilip Kumar would not have become the crown of the Hindi film industry. In all this talk about crossing over and not crossing over, it is important to remember one thing—that when the territorial division took place, many felt that people would not allow themselves to be divided; that one day they would come together.

In their speeches, Modi and Shah reject the nationalist Muslims who fought all that Jinnah stood for. They don't mention them at all. The way they see it, all Muslims should be recognized by what they wear, and that garb, according to them, is of one kind only—whereas, in this country, Muslims wear *dhotis* too, even *sherwanis* and suits (of course, the latter may not be in the range of Rs. 26 lakhs). Is it possible to imagine a constitution where one can reject, or exclude, the nationalist Muslim and still claim to be following Gandhi? My unequivocal reply is that it is just not possible.

During his rally in Vaishali district, the home minister, Amit Shah, not only quoted Gandhi, he also provided the date (26 September 1947) on which, he said, Gandhi had made that statement. I read the discourse Gandhi gave on that day, in the *Prarthana Pravachan*. It turned out that the date given by the home minister was correct—Gandhi did speak on that day—but the statement Shah read out was not; it was not part of the discourse of 26 September 1947. In that day's discourse, Gandhi shared with the audience an account of his conversation with a respected *vaidya* named Gurudutt who had come from Pakistan to meet him. In the conversation, Gurudutt tells Gandhi, 'I did not heed your advice, I came away.'

What advice of Gandhi did Gurudutt not heed? Gandhiji was telling people that wherever they were, they should be fighting against the injustices being committed by their government—even if it meant dying in the effort.

In that day's discourse, Gandhi mentions a term, 'fifth columnist', which is used to describe those people who secretly aid the enemy of their country through activities that sabotage it from within. It is important to mention this section of Gandhiji's discourse of 26 September 1947, so that Modi and Shah realize that Gandhi never said anything to the effect that Hindus and Sikhs could come over to India from Pakistan whenever they wanted. What had said was this:

> *Looking upon Hindus in Pakistan and Muslims in India as fifth columnists, as unworthy of trust, will not do. If they are disloyal to Pakistan while living there, we cannot speak for just one side. If we look upon the Muslims living here as fifth columnists, will the Hindus and Sikhs living in Pakistan be also considered fifth columnists? This will not do. Those living there, who no longer want to live there, are welcome to come here. To give them jobs, look after their comfort becomes the most important duty of our union government. But it certainly cannot be that they continue to be there and become little spies, working for us, not for Pakistan. This would never do, and I would not be party to it.*

Gandhi was completely opposed to any suggestion about doubting the nationality of minority Hindus in Pakistan and minority Muslims in India. Gandhi never said: Recognize Muslims by their clothes.

Towards the end of his discourse of 26 September 1947, Gandhi mentioned one more thing which Amit Shah seems to have missed—*Satyameva jayate, nanritam;* truth alone triumphs, not untruth.

About a week before this, in his discourse of 18 September 1947, Gandhi said: 'Assume that all Muslims in Pakistan are bad. So what? My only advice to you is, let India remain the ocean in which the filth is swept away. We cannot be doing bad things because someone else is doing them.'

What I really want is for Modi to express his 'mann ki baat' to Gandhi; to imagine he is addressing the Mahatma as he reads his prayer discourses. The prime minister's hands will start shaking and his lips will start twitching. He will be able to see how, after being cast aside by the people and by politicians, Gandhiji was still able to get on his feet, stand alone—now journeying from Delhi to Noakhali, now to Bihar. Experimenting once again with his beloved principles of ahimsa and truth, although he knew he was putting his life in danger. Gandhiji's final effort to bring these principles centre stage claimed his life.

If he does turn to Gandhi, if he does address the Mahatma, the prime minister will not be able to deny the ugly truth behind why he, Modi, gave the very person lauding Gandhi's killer, Godse, as a patriot the Lok Sabha ticket from Bhopal in 2019, and why she still sits in Parliament with him. And why he, Modi, has in his party people like Amitabh Sinha, who, during a debate on TV Today, said, in response to a direct question from Kanhaiya Kumar, that he would not say anything against Godse.

I am certain that after reading Gandhi's prayer discourses with an honest heart, Modi will go back to the same Ramlila Ground and say: 'The name of this ground is connected with the name of Rama; Rama's name is connected with truth, and Gandhi's name is also connected with truth. I have taken the names of both Rama and Gandhi and lied. I seek the forgiveness of 130 crore Indians.'

What We Have Today in India Is Truly the 'Dark Age' of Journalism

After Gautam Adani took over the TV news channel NDTV, Ravish Kumar tendered his resignation in December 2022. This is an abridged version of his farewell speech.

There was never a golden age in Indian journalism. But it was never as bad as it is now. Every good aspect of journalism is being destroyed rapidly. This was expected. But what we have today is truly the 'dark age' of journalism. There are numerous news channels in India, but all of them have compromised on their ethics and become cheer leaders of those in power. Our media ecosystem has been gutted and demolished.

Yet, everyone claims to be a journalist today. Especially those who are close to and even aligned with the powerful. These faces and establishments ironically are the very reason journalism is being trampled upon in this country. They claim to do good journalism. I implore you to be sceptical of them. These unquestioning journalists and even the government want to shove *their* definition of journalism down your throat.

At this stage, I do not want to say much about the institution I belonged to because you cannot be objective while you are emotional. Emotions often overpower facts. So it is better we leave emotions aside.

I have many interesting memories of NDTV, where I spent almost 27 years. I find it tough to thank one person. When your professional journey has been a contribution of many people, how can you thank only one? I know that many former and current colleagues and collaborators see a part of them in me, and rightfully so. I have taken something from everyone and I am grateful.

When a bride leaves her maternal home, she pines for that home even as she steps away. I feel like that bride today. Perhaps this is the moment to soak in that feeling. I shall talk about NDTV in a more equivocal tone some day in the future.

NDTV taught me that TV is made by teams. After anchors became stars, this concept was a bit shaken. But even today, I believe that your work is only as good as your team.

In August 1996, I joined NDTV formally as a translator. But I had been working there already for some time. My work was to read all the hand-written letters viewers sent. They addressed their letters to anchors of different programmes. While reading them, I saw the creation of

TV audiences in the country. My job was to make a report out of those letters and hand it to the producers of every show. I was a daily wage worker back then and got paid accordingly.

I feel like I still do the same work. Even today, thousands of you write to me. I still get hand-written letters from you. I read most of them and respond to as many as I can. I bare myself in front of you all, because I want to be honest about how I feel. If I censored my thoughts, that would mean being dishonest to you. In one way, I think I have come full circle. I'm still reading viewers' feedback letters.

I have lived my life in the midst of all of your suggestions, responses, anticipation, criticisms and even the occasional rebuke. This brought me close to you all. When I was amidst you, I didn't really live for myself. Now, I hope I will find time for that.

I feel like the bird that has lost its nest because someone else snatched it away. But the bird still has the vast sky at its disposal.

I used to translate many reports and stories of correspondents from English to Hindi. Then I became a reporter and produced a daily report called 'Ravish Ki Report'. Someone whose work was to read letters became the group editor. That was possible only at NDTV.

And today, that person tenders his resignation.

There are many powerful people who hold the strings to this institution, so it was obvious that this day would arrive. But now that the day has come, it feels sorrowful.

I just hope that when you evaluate me, you do not pity my humble beginnings. I am not like those who seek sympathy by flaunting their humble beginnings. They suddenly talk about a childhood spent as a petty tea-seller, even as they take expensive flights. I do not think of my journey as an extraordinary one. In this country, everyone has had a tough life. Just talk to the families of the patients admitted to the All India Institutes of Medical Sciences (AIIMS). You will realize they have to scale mountains we can only imagine. In comparison, our miseries are miniscule.

I want to talk to you about TV audiences. Of late, we have all witnessed institutions crash and waves of hatred engulf societies. But I have seen a new institution take shape—citizenship. Whenever NDTV gave me an opportunity, I tried to work for you. And I filled up such an opportunity with your stories.

You have a massive claim on me. You created a newsroom for me in your homes and in your minds.

All around the world, audiences have come forward to help me. You didn't ask me for money to do this, or do it as a favour. Many people recorded my videos, helped me with research. Each of my episodes is a testament to your cooperation. You provided me with information, reprimanded me for my mistakes and included yourselves in my programmes.

Experts, students, expats and Indians were viewers but also my co-passengers, and they became journalists of sorts. While doing so, they were saving a small island of journalism.

In that sense, I saw the making of a TV audience and their complete disintegration. And now, I see them stand up as an institution again.

You have translated my work into different languages. Resources have not been available to me always, but you have ensured I have access to them. [My show] 'Prime Time' was your Prime Time. If the show ever fell short, you were prompt to show your disappointment. Audiences have been my regular editors. I always say a person is a sum of all those around him. It is because of you as audience that Ravish Kumar stands here today.

Thanks to your support, several journalists find themselves on YouTube and Twitter. When you subscribe to websites, you keep them afloat.

When democratic institutions were weak and courts appeared weak, you stood strong. In these times, you are the biggest institution of journalism. Journalism today lives among enlightened audiences, not in lofty institutions. Your biggest contribution to our times is that you still stand by those journalists who ask tough questions.

There might be forces who muzzle the voice of the people, cover it with religious hatred, and kill democracy. But some of you give me hope. Because even if democracy dies, the desire for a functioning democracy survives. All thanks to you, responsible audiences.

In these tough times, I feel grateful for those elderly women who pinched my cheek in adoration, for people who gifted me potted plants and gave me nutritious sattu, to ensure I stayed healthy. Some held umbrellas over my head to shield me from oppressive heat, and others slyly put expensive pens in my pocket.

That is why I want to think of all of you today. I would have been nothing without all of you. Many times, I have felt like your representative, and not the representative of my organization. I was given a lot of freedom to work. I guarded this freedom as if my life depended on it because I knew I was being watched by you, learned audiences. I ensured I did not err or become arrogant because that would take away my freedom.

I stood at the crease like a batsman in a test match, even as the world changed in front of me. But someone just ended the match and changed the rules.

Every nation has people who take the audiences for granted, and there are some in India as well. If they claim to be giving you facts, it means they want to throw some paise at you while pocketing many rupees and dollars themselves. If some journalists and news outfits try to expose the wrong-doing of these big players, they are slapped with a battery of lawsuits. And the same players then claim glibly that they care about meaningful journalism.

Why can't many brilliant journalists who work in Hindi share their views with the world? I have been amazed at the depth of their knowledge, but they were never accorded the status they deserved.

In India, [the most respected] journalists are those who work in the English media. So I tried consciously to bring respectability to Hindi journalism so that this language remained important. I tried to make people from all over India fall in love with my Hindi. My mother tongue is Bhojpuri, not Hindi. I walked from the village of Bhojpuri to the massive city of Hindi.

I want to thank all those people from non-Hindi speaking parts of the country who enriched my Hindi. They translated my work into their languages and they also translated their texts into Hindi for me! I often felt like I was in a caravan where many joined the journey and walked shoulder to shoulder.

But I don't mean for this to turn into a wrestling match between Hindi and English journalism. It is important that I acknowledge the many contributions of English-language journalists in my life.

Every day, when I shared time with you, my audience, I was moved by your belief in journalists and amazed by your deep understanding of issues. You had so much to say. It is what the government should be listening to.

Journalists are meant to be the medium that takes your voice to the highest levels. I always tried to see the nation through your eyes. Your activism keeps Indian democracy alive. Shaheen Bagh and the farmers' protests strengthened my belief in you. I saw you transform into responsible citizens. It is citizens like you who will make better societies in the future.

Today some believe that they control all major aspects of our society. They believe citizens are dispensable. The media is dead and the political opposition is struggling.

All of that is true. But such a state is not eternal. One day people will overcome their hatred. They will look to build a new society, and they will think of journalism then.

I learnt to read, write and speak at NDTV. I leant how to wear good clothes and wear a tie. I didn't get to learn to dance, because there was never a free moment.

Today I want to specially remember my female colleagues. They taught me sincerity, hard work and ethics. They broadened my understanding of social issues. My journey includes the experiences of many women and girls. My partner, my daughters, my mother and my sister-in-law supported me. Journalism is dominated by men and patriarchy. Their aggression was suffocating. Such aggression kills creativity and thought. My female colleagues saved me from such aggression.

If you are just starting out in this field, I would advise you to be courteous to your female colleagues. Admit and admire their capacity.

India's media space has changed. My heart goes out to those young Indians who are paying millions of rupees to train to be journalists because they have to work as agents of the State. There is no institution left for ethical journalists.

The few who are still trying to be what journalists should be are feeling suffocated if they haven't yet exited the profession. Many have told me that they look at journalism as just another profession now, something they do to earn a living. There is no other motivation.

A scared journalist produces a dead citizenry. So [I would urge you], speak up fearlessly. You are citizens of a country where people walked barefoot to bring the mighty British to their knees. There is no reason to not trust you. You will break away from the shackles of unethical media messaging. You have to fight this. You can't walk with your head held high if you do not fight. If you do not fight, you will be citizens of an independent country, but will remain slaves of a sold-out media. Beware of such a situation. Under the garb of laws, the rights of people are being undermined, so that all that is illegal appears to be legal.

At this point, my future is uncertain. The only certainty is hope.

(Translated by Raksha Kumar)

Big Money Is No Guarantee of a Healthy, Accountable and Free Media*

'Trust in Modi was not born out of newspaper headlines or through shining faces on TV. I have given my life, every moment, for the people of this country.' This is what Prime Minister Narendra Modi said about himself in February 2023 when the opposition demanded answers over the Hindenburg report and Gautam Adani.†

Perhaps the prime minister's conceit would contain a modicum of truth if the media had questioned his silence, and if he had actually answered the allegations levelled against his government. Instead, we had the PM's speech in which he told the Lok Sabha: 'Will the 80 crore countrymen who get free ration ever trust those making false allegations?'

---

*This is an edited and updated version of an essay that first appeared on *Newslaundry* in July 2023.

†In a report released in January 2023, US short seller *Hindenburg* Research had accused the Adani Group of accounting fraud and stock price manipulation. Gautam Adani, Chairman of the Adani Group, is widely believed to have a close relationship with the Narendra Modi regime.

And so, with this single speech, the prime minister of 'the world's largest democracy' shook off all demands for accountability.

For the last ten years, 'Godi media' anchors have been in the PM's service, casting journalism into the gutter in the process. Yet, the same PM said he owes them nothing. This is the boast of a leader who has not held a single press conference in nine years, a leader who has not been questioned by the 'Godi media' for nine years.

It is impossible to take the media out of Modi, and Modi out of the media. These lap-dog sections of the media remain silent towards him. If they speak, they speak only *for* him. When a social worker or journalist outside their cult of Modi worship gets respect in foreign countries, they call it an 'anti-India' conspiracy. But when the PM gets respect in the same countries, they describe it as a 'Vishwaguru' moment—a glorious moment when India's name—Narendra Modi's name—rings across the globe.

The near decade since 2014 belongs as much to the 'Godi media' as it does to Modi. These channels have different names but the same content. The packaging is poor, their stories are similar, and they've shattered many myths in the process.

'No Money' Is No Longer an Excuse

Before 2014, we believed TV journalism was haunted by the ghost called 'No money'. News channel owners, who usually weren't journalists, were running out of funds, we were told. We could not expect quality; we should understand their constraints. Everything was done in the hope of gaining TRPs—it had to be; the alternative was shutting down the channel entirely.

Most of these owners didn't really care about journalism. But even otherwise good-intentioned but 'helpless' owners of established channels would follow their example, or they wouldn't get advertisements. This was how an alibi was created for poor content—the myth of the market.

And now this myth has been busted. The new owners of Big Media are Mukesh Ambani and Gautam Adani. Ambani already owns many channels and Adani is launching several news channels this year [2023]. Given the number of channels and the wealth these gentlemen have between them, the ghost 'No money' should have fled. But why aren't we seeing the effect of these funds on content? Why aren't their wealth and business acumen improving the poor state of TV journalism, especially when these expenses are far lower than their other businesses? What examples have Ambani and Adani's channels set in journalism? What have they done that is new, or even spectacular?

These are my questions, and the answers are simple.

There are two essential and basic conditions for good journalism: courage and questions. Without courage, you cannot question. Without questions, courage has no meaning.

So, you cannot change the content of 'Godi media' with just business skills and money. You need courage and you need to question. Instead, Ambani and Adani join the queue that already includes the head honchos of the corporate media. A queue where everyone is timid.

This has been the biggest change in the mainstream media over the last ten years. Their content isn't influenced by the owners, it is influenced by the 'unknown owner' of these owners. We cannot expect these channels to ask questions like *The Telegraph* does. Merely opening a channel or launching a newspaper or magazine does not make one a journalist. The content of these channels and papers tells us all we need to know about the relationship they have with the Modi government. When journalists protest in Delhi against attacks on their peers, take a look at how many journalists from these channels and papers are in attendance.

I don't consider *The Wire*, *Caravan*, *Scroll*, *Newslaundry*,

Alt News, *NewsClick*, *The News Minute*, *Boomlive* and *Article 14* as alternatives to the mainstream media. That line of thinking frees the mainstream media from guilt. These stellar institutions should be seen as individual efforts. Their names should not be brought up during the 'Godi media' debate by claiming that they are also products of this era. Because they are not—the government does not give them ads. Corporate ads are rarely available to them. They aren't the startups aided by the government.

What we should talk about are the media houses that get crores of public money in the form of government or government-sponsored ads. Why aren't they practising what we understand as journalism? If journalism is not possible, if it isn't viable, then why are India's richest opening news channels?

The two richest industrialists in the world have thrown their money at the 'Godi media' which operates in the name of journalism. So we must conclude that there is a market for journalism per se, that it is good business. But the conviction and satisfaction, the pleasure of making a product from the heart is missing.

Let me ask you this: Why don't young, educated people from startup incubators think of a media startup? It is because they know that they will not be free to create independent content in the media. Without freedom, journalism is not possible; what is created without freedom can be many things, but not journalism.

But 'Godi media' has developed just such a model—it runs in the name of journalism, but its product has no connection to journalism.

During the *NDTV* takeover, Gautam Adani had said that India 'does not have a single [outlet] to compare with the *Financial Times* or *Al Jazeera*'. He had wondered why this was the case, because, he had implied, there was no dearth of money. Adani should know that journalism isn't driven by money.

We must remember that it is the same gentleman, Gautam Adani, who had demanded that the *Financial Times* take down a report on his empire's 'offshore funding'. The *Financial Times* had refused to do this, saying that it stood by its reporting.

Several global media houses, for the most part, have this level of integrity and courage. So some form of journalism still survives there. It has little to do with money.

Indian news channel owners buy expensive cars for their anchors, but will not post reporters anywhere outside the cities where their studios are. If Adani wants to create a global media brand, he could start here.

We hear that Modi would like a global Indian media

brand too. But look at what happened to *Doordarshan*. In the nine years of Modi's India, it is flush with funds and it is not a shadow even of what it used to be 15 or 20 years ago. Where does the massive public money it gets from the government go? It is used up in actively playing the 'Godi media' game.

Outliving a Purpose

The 'Godi media' factory does not produce questions for the government. It manufactures weapons to target those who do ask questions, calling them traitors or terrorists.

But a lot of viewers have begun to get bored of this. Is this a case of diminishing returns? Probably. But the circus will continue.

At a glance, the scene seems to be changing. Old faces are switching from one channel to the other, new channels are launching with brand-new faces. But they are repackaged versions of the same product, all performing the same task. It is like the mafia movies from the golden days of cinema: an old gang leader is eliminated but a new one soon takes his place. The empire continues.

Yet credibility is so low that ministers are giving interviews to social media influencers—a throwback to the time when Modi picked the Bollywood actor Akshay Kumar to interview him in 2019. They wouldn't have to do this if Adani and Ambani's channels and anchors had built credibility for themselves.

We should remember that the opposition took too long to understand the power wielded by Modi's 'Godi media'. It finally happened when Rahul Gandhi, during the Bharat Jodo Yatra, established his press conferences as an alternative to these news channels. He challenged journalists, saying, 'You cannot ask this question of the PM, but you can ask me.' They did ask him—and he answered.

Of course, the 'Godi media' all but ignored Rahul's yatra. Now that the yatra is over, Rahul doesn't mention the 'Godi media' as much in his speeches. And while he showed some courage and imagination, Congress governments have learned no lessons from him. They are now giving their ads to these same channels, despite their shabby treatment of their leader. Imagine the irony: Modi's ministers are flocking towards influencers, while Congress governments are turning to the 'Godi media' with their ads.

Meanwhile, the end of journalism is being celebrated.